EXCELSIOR SPRINGS
HAUNTED HAVEN

HING RIVER, EXCELSIOR SPRINGS, MO.

Along the banks of the Fishing River, pictured in this c. 1910 postcard, the first local mineral water spring was discovered and the township of Excelsior Springs was born. (From the private collection of Betty Bissell.)

ON THE FRONT COVER: This photograph of Tryst Falls is from the 1880s or 1890s. The location is identified on the back of the photograph as Fishing River Falls. Also written on the back is "Trysting place James Boys, Clay Co. near Kearney." Although rumors continue to persist, descendents of the first owners of this land concur the area was never a hangout for the infamous James Gang. This site is, however, the location of a heart-wrenching murder and reportedly ghostly apparitions. (With permission from the digital collection from the Missouri Valley Special Collections, Kansas City Missouri Public Library, Kansas City, Missouri.)

ON THE BACK COVER: Siloam Springs is considered by many the birthplace of Excelsior Springs. This building was part of a larger complex designed in 1917 by landscape architect George E. Kessler and architect Henry F. Hoit. Siloam Spring Pavilion and the Sulpho-Saline Pavilion stood side by side. The style of these structures is highly reminiscent of the neoclassical architectural style utilized during the World's Fair of 1904 in St. Louis, Missouri. George Kessler was also the landscape architect for the 1904 World's Fair. (From the private collection of Betty Bissell.)

EXCELSIOR SPRINGS
HAUNTED HAVEN

Janet R. Reed and the
Excelsior Springs Museum and Archives

ARCADIA
PUBLISHING

Published by Arcadia Publishing
Charleston, South Carolina

Printed in the United States of America

Library of Congress Control Number: 2010934146

For all general information contact Arcadia Publishing at:
Telephone 843-853-2070
Fax 843-853-0044
E-mail sales@arcadiapublishing.com
For customer service and orders:
Toll-Free 1-888-313-2665

Visit us on the Internet at www.arcadiapublishing.com

*This book is dedicated to my husband, Don Reed; my son,
Joe Kline, who assisted greatly; and Kate Fields, who pointed me
to Excelsior Springs.*

CONTENTS

Acknowledgments

This history would not have been possible without the support and contributions of so many parties. Boundless thanks to the following:

Organizations

Clay County Archives
210 East Franklin Street
Liberty, MO 64068-1790
Phone: (816) 781-3611

Clay County Museum and Historical Society
16 North Main Street
Liberty, MO 64068
Phone: (816) 792-1849

Downtown Excelsior Partnership
PO Box 513
Excelsior Springs, MO 64024
Phone: (816) 522-4362

Excelsior Springs Historic Preservation
  Commission
Hall of Waters, 201 E. Broadway
Excelsior Springs, MO 64024
Phone: (816) 630-9594

Excelsior Springs Museum and Archives
101 East Broadway Street
Excelsior Springs, MO 64024-2513
Phone: (816) 630-0101

Jesse James Farm & Museum
21216 Jesse James Farm Road
Kearney, MO 64060-9343
(816) 628-4859

Kansas City Public Library
14 West 10 Street
Kansas City, MO 64105
(816) 701-3400

Mid-Continent Public Library: Excelsior
  Springs Branch
1460 Kearney Road
Excelsior Springs, MO 64024-1746
(816) 630-6721

Ray County Historical Society and Museum
901 West Royle Street
Richmond, MO 64085-1545
(816) 776-2305

Thomas Hart Benton Home & Studio State
  Historic Site
3616 Belleview Avenue
Kansas City, MO 64111
Phone: (816) 931-5722

Harry S. Truman Library & Museum
500 US Highway 24
Independence, MO 64050-1798
(816) 268-8200

Special Projects Associates
418 Wildwood Street
Excelsior Springs, MO 64024

Paranormal Adventures USA
www.paranormaladventuresusa.com

PARANORMAL TEAMS ASSISTING

Kansas City Paranormal Investigations
Paranormal Activity Investigators
Paranormal Encounter Documentation and Research Organization
Paranormal Research Investigators

GREG ELLISON COLLECTION

We are grateful for the use of the Ellison Collection photographs for this publication. The majority of these photographs of Jesse James, his family, and his gang have never appeared in a publication before this time. It is also the first publication to present the Jesse James portion of the Ellison Collection as a whole.

INTRODUCTION

FOLLOW THE RULES

The following instructions are not a set of rules on how to conduct a paranormal investigation. Many well-known authors have already done an excellent job of writing guidebooks for new investigators and ghost-hunting teams. Notable among these publications are Troy Taylor's *The Ghost Hunter's Guidebook* and R.H. Southall's *How to Be a Ghost Hunter*. This list should instead be considered a set of guidelines for paranormal researchers on how to conduct themselves professionally and present their follow-up documentation in a way that is conducive to generating a mutual respect between ghost hunters and the world at large.

Paranormal research has long been considered a pseudoscience at best and something evil or demonic at worst. Until recently, those searching out ghostly experiences had to do so in utmost secret, hiding their intentions and often their findings from the world, lest they be labeled deluded and outright crazy. But happily, this is frequently no longer the case. Thanks to those who have bravely blazed the trails before us and also through Hollywood studios creating movie after movie and a string of television shows based (although often loosely) on the ghost-hunting experience, much of the world is now accepting of the paranormal adventurer.

Acceptance by the world does not equal entitlement by ghost hunters or paranormal teams to go wherever they please and conduct research without first having the utmost respect for the location, the property owners, the history, and the community in which the investigation takes place. Ghost hunting does not occur in a vacuum; it is the culmination of shared experiences by eyewitnesses, documentation from investigations, and thorough research into the history surrounding the haunting.

RULE 1: NEVER INVESTIGATE A LOCATION WITHOUT THE PERMISSION OF THE PROPERTY OWNER

No ghost hunters worth their salt would step foot on someone else's property without first obtaining permission to do so. Without permission, there is no possibility of any validation of any of the evidence, no matter how demonstrative, you might gather. Those who dare to cross this line risk not only damaging their reputation and the credibility of their team, but they will in all likelihood close the location to any future paranormal research, even if the site proves to be a veritable hotbed of paranormal activity.

RULE 2: THOROUGHLY RESEARCH THE HISTORY OF THE HAUNTED LOCATION

It is easy to fall into the trap of merging the findings of an investigation with history received from property owners, amateur historians, and eyewitness accounts. Do not assume that everyone is accurately relating the history of a haunted location. Rumors have often been distorted into facts, and speculation can twist itself into the hearts and minds of those tasked with overseeing their beloved historic sites. Take the time to visit local libraries, museums, historical societies, and newspaper archives to research any key events that may have taken place in or near the location in question. Even if you are one of the lucky few to capture photographs, voices, and other ghostly phenomena during a paranormal investigation, if you publish inaccurate or incomplete history with your results, not only will the history fall into question, but so will the entire investigation, the results, your team, and any future investigations of the same location. Beth Cooper, cofounder of Ghost Tours of Kansas/Missouri and Paranormal Adventures USA, states it best by telling her employees and tour guests, "Without history, there are no hauntings."

Rule 3: Respect the Community, Their Values, Their History, and Their Wishes

The majority of paranormal activity can be tied to a death or multiple deaths in the past at a given location. Often the haunting is based on a series of traumatic events that have left lasting impressions on the lives of those in the community. While conducting research where results are measured by scientific means, it is easy to overlook the human component to the phenomenon. A good paranormal researcher should also take care to realize that the story you may repeat when relaying the history of a haunted location is also someone else's property—it is their story that they have been kind enough to share with you. It could be the story of their ancestors, recently deceased relatives, or of an unfortunate event in the annuals of their hometown. While you may be merely passing through, the location or the area in question is their home and often, as in the case of a haunting at a business, the source of their livelihood. Respect should be your mantra, especially when publishing your findings!

One

HEALING WATERS

The first residents of Excelsior Springs must have been drawn by the sheer beauty of the natural surroundings, for although deep ravines with rushing waters and steep embankments display nature at its finest, they also made life extremely difficult for early settlers who were attempting to clear the land and grow the crops necessary for their survival.

The birth story of Excelsior Springs begins with a miraculous healing and a mineral water spring, but early tales are so steeped in myth, magic, miracles, and lore that it is now very difficult to discern the true facts from the multitude of fictional stories.

"Once upon a time," begins the introduction to *The Waters of Excelsior Springs, Valley of Vitality*. In all likelihood, the inclusion of an urban legend in the introduction section of this historical reference book was necessary due to the tale becoming engrained in the hearts and minds of decades' worth of tourists to the area. The tale begins by truthfully describing the majestic beauty of the valley area around the Fishing River. The book depicts the lush rugged hills with grand trees and deep canyons flowing with sparking waters and later factually relates the intricate details on the many flowing springs and the industries that arose based on the healing properties of the waters.

Then the tale of an Indian hunter by the name of Wapoo begins. According to local legend, Wapoo discovered both the valley and the healing properties provided by the mineral springs in the area by chance when he became weary from being wounded while hunting. Wapoo was exhausted and thirsty and struggling to continue on when he happened to catch the sounds of a rushing stream nearby. He managed to press on until he reached the shore of the stream and drank from the refreshing waters.

Wapoo immediately noticed that the water on his lips had an odd taste. At the same time, he spotted a reddish stain on several of the stones along the embankment of the stream. Knowing the danger signs, Wapoo was concerned the water may be poisonous, which contradicted the overall alleviation from pain he was beginning to experience. He then washed his wounds in the uncertain waters and lay down to rest.

Wapoo felt his wounds heal at an amazing rate and gave thanks to the Almighty. According to the story, he called the water a "gift of life." When Wapoo returned was reunited with his tribe, he informed them of the beautiful place with the healing waters. The legend continues that Wapoo's tribe began to regularly return to the place where he had been healed after completion of the hunting season. The hunters following Wapoo's example came to refresh themselves and drink from the same healing waters.

And to take the fantasy to a whole new level, this publication later references an earlier publication from the 1940s multiplying the number of healings among Chief Wapoo's fighting men. Tribal warriors were believed to be healed of their battle wounds by cleansing in the iron mineral water. "Wapoo related that he was called the Keeper of the Springs, and that it was his duty to keep the springs clear of brush and weeds and free from contamination of any kind." The narrative talks of a total of 10 mineral springs called Peace Valley Springs by the native inhabitants to the Fishing River Valley. According to the fable, each of the springs was overseen by a beautiful Indian maiden.

Another far more plausible version of the city's birth can be found printed in *Excelsior Springs, America's Haven of Health*. "Early pioneers called it the 'pizen' spring—and let it alone." At the center of this version is an African American farmer by the name of Travis Mellion. His daughter was suffering from scrofula, and out of desperation he had her drink from the reddish waters flowing from the spring.

Earlier, he had been talking with a group of hunters about his daughter's battle with this unfortunate skin disease. He further relayed all of the various treatments attempted so far that were unable to offer the poor child any relief. Someone in the group began to recount the medicinal properties of a mineral spring in the area. It was suggested that Travis Mellion offer the water to his daughter to drink and that she should bathe in the waters as well. Although he was concerned about the possible outcome, he had tried everything else, so the suggestion of ingesting the waters was probably a last resort. He gave the water to his daughter to drink, and the girl experienced a speedy recovery and soon was showing little trace of the affliction that had brought so much grief to her life. All that remained were a few small scars to remind the Mellions of the tragedy that earlier befell them.

In the midst of these tales are clearly trickles of the truth. The following is an abbreviated version compiled from an article written for the *Daily Standard* of Excelsior Springs, Missouri, on July 25, 1940, by Gordon Clevenger, the grandson of Richard Clevenger, and reprinted in *The Clevenger Families of Ray County*, MO by Carol and Barbara Proffitt with typing and editing help from Virginia Mills.

Richard Clevenger and his two sons journeyed up the Mississippi and Missouri Rivers from Tennessee with others by boat to become some of Ray and Clay Counties' first settlers. Richard and his wife, Sarah (Sally), were raised and married in Tennessee.

The women stayed with the supplies on the boat, while the men traversed the riverbanks pulling the boat along with them. They had stopped at Lexington for a wagon and oxen to carry them forward while searching for a place to settle their homes. It has been said that a bear actually led them to the place where they decided to settle. The best way at the time to discern where the water would be safest to drink was to track a bear to his watering hold.

Richard Clevenger chose land near the fresh water to purchase a 160-acre tract. These early settlers built their homes to the east of present-day Excelsior Springs. Some years later, when the properties of the mineral waters were fully understood, homes would be constructed on the farmland along the Fishing River in the area where Excelsior Springs can be found today. Additional details on the Clevenger family can be found in the chapter relating to the Battle of Fredericksburg.

Once the key founding figures of Excelsior Springs were settled in the area, their lives were focused on the mineral springs, their healing properties, and the masses drawn to drink from the curative waters. Among these key figures was Fred Kugler, a German farmer who decided to use the mineral spring water to treat his rheumatic knees and a running sore on his leg that had been caused by a gunshot wound received during the Civil War. After his remarkably quick recovery occurred, word of the amazing healing properties of the mineral spring began to spread.

In 1880, Anthony Wyman and his wife, Elizabeth, were the owners of 40 acres of land along the banks of the Fishing River on the site where the first spring was discovered. John Van Buren Flack, a minister from Missouri City, heard of the miraculous healings and began working with the Wymans. Together they had a sample of the water sent away to be analyzed for its mineral properties. Planning ahead, their next step was to plat the Wyman land into the future city plots. Then they wisely began to advertise the mineral waters to the world at large. It was on this platted land that Rev. J.V.B. Flack, DD, built his home and his church, the Church of Christ in Christian Union. This historic church, which played a vital role in the creation and expansion of Excelsior Springs, still stands on a lot at the northwest corner of East Excelsior Street and Kugler Lane.

Built in 1881, the church was originally a simple white frame structure. Along with founding the town, Reverend Flack became one of the founders of the Christian Union movement. Reverend Flack himself seeded the church building fund by personally donating the land and a good portion of the money required for the first building. In 1912, funds were raised for a new brick church structure. It was named the Flack Memorial Christian Union Church.

It was Reverend Flack who chose the name "Excelsior" for the newly discovered mineral spring from the Henry Wadsworth Longfellow poem of the same name. The name "Excelsior" from the poem later became part of the name for the entire city. The poem is about a young man on a winter's journey holding up a banner bearing the single word "Excelsior." The young man passes up all assistance from those reaching out to him and instead journeys on, only to be found later, frozen to death in the snow, still holding tight to the banner.

The name of this first spring was later changed to Siloam Spring. Today the location of Siloam Spring can be found under the front steps of the historic Hall of Waters. Details on the history and haunting experiences at the Hall of Waters can be found in chapter three.

News of the miraculous healing waters continued to spread rapidly beyond the town, for within one short year, nearly 200 new homes were built around the area of the spring. Many more people continued to arrive. Newcomers camped out in tents or traveled in covered wagons to experience the healing waters for themselves and their loved ones. Cures for almost every type of disease known to man were accredited to the waters' healing properties. By July 1881, the local community was incorporated with hotels, boardinghouses, schools, an opera house, livery stables, and many stores. Soon a second mineral spring was discovered and was named Empire Spring. The name of the spring was later changed to Regent Spring and was an iron manganese spring located just south of the future location for the Elms Resort & Spa.

It was not much longer before a third, fourth, and eventually over 40 natural springs were discovered in the Excelsior Springs area. Excelsior Springs could now make claim to having the world's greatest group of mineral waters. Particularly unusual is the fact that these springs included two of the world's only six iron-manganese springs. Other types of mineral springs were saline-super, soda-bicarbonate, and calcium bicarbonate. The abundance and variety of mineral waters within the city set the area apart and above the other healing-water resorts of the era. The vast majority of healing water spring resorts rarely possessed more than one type of mineral water treatment.

Industries grew quickly, all based around the restorative properties of the natural spring waters and providing for the hopeful throngs of ill and dying masses arriving to partake from them. Campsites, boardinghouses, and hotels soon progressed into extensive resorts catering to well-to-do visitors. Local hotels and resorts were equipped with mineral spas, and clinics had hydrotherapy treatments and their own doctors who could prescribe a variety of treatments.

The healing springs gave a renewed spirit to many, and their reputations for miraculous results grew, bringing thousands upon thousands of weary travelers from around the world to this tucked-away retreat town. It has been estimated that during the boom years of Excelsior Springs,

EXCELSIOR SPRINGS: HAUNTED HAVEN

between 1880 and the early 1960s, many years saw over 20,000 visitors make the trek in search of a life-renewing and in some cases a life-saving cure.

The local newspaper, the *Daily Standard*, regularly gave space to testimonials of the wondrous healing properties of the spring waters. One such article, published on January 28, 1947, tells of a Mrs. Baxter, the wife of a honeybee farmer from Blair, Nebraska, who arrived in Excelsior Springs in a wheelchair due to advanced arthritis. Within just a few weeks of taking regular treatments of mineral water baths and drinking curative waters, she was seen free of her wheelchair walking in the downtown district. She was able to return to her home in perfect health. She was quoted as saying she was grateful to the neighbor her who informed her of Excelsior Springs and urged she travel to try the restorative treatments.

Within a short span of time, the waters from the various springs were in such high demand that they were bottled and shipped to customers around the world. While the waters in the area gave health, the frequent flooding from the Fishing River also destroyed many of the city's early buildings and homes on several occasions. The following is a listing of a few more recent examples: in 1941, water rose to the 32-foot mark on the sides of buildings along the banks of the Fishing River and caused nearly $10,000 damage to the Hall of Waters; in 1943, another flood completely filled the lower level of the Hall of Waters, which included the boiler rooms and the bottling works; in 1969, the flooding was so deep that the downtown business area was immersed in water, and homes were forced to be evacuated as well; and in 1974, flooding damaged four city bridges and 50 homes, broke water and sewer mains, and caused damage to two floors at the Hall of Waters.

While many left feeling relaxed, cleansed, and refreshed, for countless others who had journeyed to the emerging town, the end of their life's journey was in Excelsior Springs. The sick and diseased continued to fill every hotel, boardinghouse, private home, and campsite available. Funeral homes and undertakers founded thriving businesses to administer to needs of the dearly departed on the final leg of their journey to the hereafter.

The reader may speculate on the various reasons as to why Excelsior Springs is home to so many lingering spirits from beyond. Perhaps it is the combination of the hills, natural springs, and the wide variety of mineral deposits in the area. Or perhaps the residual energies resulted from the still-resonating emotions of the throngs of diseased yet hopeful souls traveling across the country seeking a cure from the healing waters, only to be met with disappointment and death. But perhaps that the main reason for the excessive number of unexplained ghostly activities reported in this area can be linked to the indelible spirit of the residents of Excelsior Springs themselves. After growing a community in the midst of this Edenic setting and with great care tending to the needs of hundreds of thousands of seriously ill travelers, Excelsior Springs inhabitants continue on for generation after generation as positive, upbeat, welcoming, and friendly as ever. Visitors may even find themselves returning again and again, lingering among those peaceful hills and hesitant to leave Excelsior Springs behind.

Two

HAUNTED HOTELS

THE ALBANY HOTEL

In Excelsior Springs, just as in the majority of Midwestern towns of past, segregation was viewed as a common function of society and was a generally accepted part of every day life. And, since illness makes no dissimilarity between race, creed, or color, it became necessary to provide separate hotels and medical facilities to treat all those in need who ventured into the city. It was out of this perceived need for separation that the Albany Hotel was constructed for African American visitors to Excelsior Springs seeking the curing water treatments in the area. It served as the only hotel solely dedicated to this unique segment of the population in the community.

Records show that the Albany Hotel was originally owned and operated by Mr. and Mrs. Stanford King. They chose a location for their hotel next to their already existing K.C. Steam Cleaning business. The hotel at 410–412 South Street had 25 guest rooms with electric lights and advertised itself as "neatly and comfortably furnished." The south-facing building and its shady grounds were bordered to the north by the Dry Fork of the East Fork of the Fishing River. At one time, a swinging bridge spanned the creek and led to a settlement known to locals as the "Bottoms."

By 1917, H.B. and Marie E. White were the Albany Hotel's registered owners. They also operated a barbershop on the first floor of the hotel. Over the years, the Albany had various business ventures on the first floor, including the Albany Café, a grocery store, and a feed store.

At the beginning of the 20th century, Excelsior Springs had few options available for African Americans to access the healing water therapy treatments that had made the area so famous. They could visit the Star Bath House, owned and operated by Dr. D.A. Ellett, or visit a small parlor run by W.A. and Mrs. Doxey, who were advertised as "practical bathers" and masseurs. The Star Bath House was across from the ornate Sulpho Saline Pavilion. One advertisement in the local paper promoted the Star Bath House as being able to provide all kinds of baths, including mineral, plain, mud, vapor, Turkish, shower, douche, electric, and magnetic and finished with the enticing words of "Everything First-Class."

Due to the lack of services for this particular sector of the population, the Albany Hotel eventually became home to many long-term African American residents who made their living working for the white clientele in the nearby hotels and medical clinics.

Only a portion of the original two-building complex called the Albany Hotel survives today. The smaller redbrick building at 410 South Street still faintly displays the words "Albany Hotel" in black above the second-story windows. This two-story addition was constructed between 1905 and 1907. (Author's collection.)

The foundation of the Albany and much of the original structure was extensively damaged during one of the frequent floods in Excelsior Springs and required demolition of much of the original property. All that remains today of the original two-building complex is a smaller adjacent redbrick building at 410 South Street. This two-story addition was constructed between 1905 and 1907. Visitors can still faintly read the words "Albany Hotel" painted in black above the second-story windows.

The Albany Hotel was by no stretch of the imagination grand or ostentatious. It was one of the smaller hotels in the city, sitting just one block west of several of the majestic resort buildings in the historic downtown area. Details of the original Albany Hotel appear small in comparison to the grandeur of some of the larger hotels nearby. But, when this building is compared to the entire tourism industry that flourished in the city during its boom years, the Albany Hotel was larger than the extensive number of small boardinghouses that flourished throughout the community. Some reports state that during the height of the healing springs industry, Excelsior Springs was home to 12 large resort hotels and nearly another 200 additional small hotels, motels, and boardinghouses. This simple, unassuming building became the site of one of the city's most horrendous murders and launched a manhunt that reached as far as the Kansas City area, propelling the city shortly into notoriety through headlines across the front pages of Midwestern newspapers in the early 1940s.

It was on Valentine's Day in 1940, and a man named John Brown who was living at the Albany Hotel arrived at his job as a janitor at the Beyer Theatre. The theater was packed with couples snuggling in the dark, enjoying the romance of the day, when a small six-year-old African American boy ran into the building in search of Mr. Brown and shouted, "Mama's dead!" Unbeknownst to Roy and Eleanor Monroe, the current proprietors of the Albany Hotel, the boy and his mother, Lorraine "Tiney" Sayles, had been secretly residing for some time with Mr. Brown in his room.

When the police arrived at the hotel, they interviewed the young boy, who seemed unaware of the severity of the events he had recently witnessed. The child was found quietly playing with two of the three bullets that ended the life of his mother. Of course, the bullets were immediately taken from the boy and placed into evidence. The child related that his mother had been shot once while lying on the bed. His mother had then jumped up and was shot twice more in the back. The child identified his mother's murderer as her husband, a Gen. Sylvester Sayles. He next told the police that he became worried about his mother and went to get her a drink. The child further related to the police that General Sayles was not his father and that his own father was living somewhere in Chicago, Illinois.

Next, Mr. Brown was interviewed by the police. He informed the officers that the killer, General Sayles, had shown up at the room he was sharing with the man's wife and the child at the Albany Hotel earlier in the day. Mr. Brown thought the man appeared to be calm and polite. He stated that General Sayles had promised him that he was not there to harm anyone. The exchange between the two men appeared so peaceful to Mr. Brown that, after sitting down and discussing the situation, he stated they shook hands. It was because of the nature of this civil discussion that Mr. Brown felt no reservations as he left for his job at the nearby theater shortly before the killing occurred.

It was quickly ascertained that the killer had casually walked away from the Albany Hotel after the fatal shooting of his wife and had hailed a very convenient taxi for Kansas City. It was this taxi ride that sparked off a metro-wide manhunt, for police records had uncovered that the suspected killer had previously served a year in an Oklahoma prison for assault with attempt to kill. The suspect was arrested only two days later at a boardinghouse in Kansas City, just nine blocks from the spot where he had departed the taxi. Sayles went quietly with the police and admitted to his crime. He told police his wife was frequently unfaithful and that when he left the scene of the crime he was unaware his wife had died as a result of the shooting. Sayles was later convicted of manslaughter and sentenced to serve just five years in prison.

CASTLE ROCK HOTEL
THE BALL CLINIC/SPA VIEW NURSING HOME

Construction began on the ornate Queen Anne–style Castle Rock Hotel in 1900 and continued through 1905. Situated at 120 East Bluff Street on a rocky hillside above the town, visitors to Excelsior Springs in the past could not help but take notice of the impressive Castle Rock Hotel, as it dominated the landscape directly to the north of the downtown business district. This three-story hotel featured an expansive multilevel porch and decorative corner turrets.

As with many of the major structures in Excelsior Springs, 120 East Bluff Street changed owners and business direction over the course of time. No history of Excelsior Springs would be complete without mention of the Ball Clinic and its large network, which spread out in the downtown area, including appropriating the building formerly known as Castle Rock Hotel.

In 1918, Dr. Samuel Ball began his private practice on Broadway Street in the downtown district of Excelsior Springs, and in 1919 he founded the Ball Clinic. This clinic offered an alternative to the invasive surgical and medical treatments of the day by utilizing a combination of therapies, including physical therapy, diet, hydrotherapy, chiropractic, osteopathic, and other similar methods to treat those suffering from arthritis, rheumatism, and serious chronic conditions. Integrated into the many possible treatment options for patients were the mineral waters of the area, and eventually the clinic drilled four mineral water wells of its own. The remains of the stone pillars for the Link's Soda Pavilion and Sulpho Salt Well can still be seen today standing as silent guardians over the mineral water spring near the base of the hillside.

The Ball Clinic organization grew so large that it was eventually housed in seven separate buildings and became a major employer in the area. In 1926, the Ball Clinic purchased the Castle Rock Hotel, and the clinic quickly added two more stories to the original structure and constructed a stone five-story addition to the east. During this same period of growth, the Ball Health School was erected on the nearby corner of East Broadway and Elizabeth Streets.

It may have been the massive heat wave that was sweeping across the Midwest setting record highs that aided in the destruction to one the annexes of the Ball Clinic on the fateful day of August 22, 1936. The building in question is described as a one-story brick building that originally housed the women's bathhouse, was later converted into a clinic, and was being remodeled to become an office. A massive explosion occurred that was so forceful that it shook the city and sent bricks and debris flying into the air more than a block away.

In the basement was a 24-year-old maintenance worker who was busy painting at the time of the catastrophe. He was crushed to death when the concrete support of the first floor crashed down upon him. Another employee of the health clinic was busy closing windows on the first floor when the blast occurred and was injured as he was blown approximately 15 feet through a door and out onto the street. A taxi driver in the vicinity was also slightly injured when flying bricks crashed into his car. Acting out of pure valor, he parked further down the street and rushed back to aid any possible victims left in the debris. The few people who were near the building at the time of the explosion narrowly missed being harmed by the bricks as they plummeted through the air.

The explosion caused a fire within the remains of the building, and soon a large crowd of onlookers began to gather. The street was blocked off to keep the curiosity seekers out of harm's

This historic late-1920s photograph features a front view of the Ball Medical Clinic, which was located on a hillside at 120 East Bluff Street overlooking the downtown area of Excelsior Springs. The former Castle Rock Hotel, the wooden structure on the left, was purchased by Dr. Samuel Ball in 1926. To the east on the front of the limestone building is a sign designating the addition as Dr. Ball's Health School. (From the collection of the Excelsior Springs Museum and Archives.)

This 1930s postcard features a larger health school complex. The organization grew so large that it eventually was housed in seven separate buildings. In the foreground of this postcard, small pavilions for the mineral water wells can be seen. Over time, the clinic drilled four mineral water wells of its own. The stone pillars for the Link's Soda Pavilion and Sulpho Salt Well are still visible today near the base of the hillside. (From the collection of Betty Bissell.)

way as firemen searched the ruins for the missing maintenance worker. It would be over an hour after the explosion before his lifeless body could be removed from beneath the rubble.

Less than a block away, the majestic Hall of Waters was under construction. Fortunately, the destruction caused by the explosion and the fire that followed did not damage the $1-million Works Projects Administration (WPA) development. Some speculation was raised that the construction project forced gases from the sewer lines into the buildings in the area, inciting the disaster. But another, more plausible origin can be found in the intense heat wave, with temperatures nearing the 115-degree mark, combined with the paint fumes in the enclosed basement, which could have easily been triggered by the tiniest of sparks.

Dr. Samuel Ball retired from practice in 1953 and passed away in 1956 after devoting nearly his entire adult life to aiding the seriously ill. His son C.E. Ball, who had worked by his father's side for many years, took over the management of the company. On September 1, 1958, five buildings of the former Ball Clinic, including the Castle Rock Hotel, became the Spa-View Nursing Home. This new facility boasted a capacity of 200 patient beds with experienced staff to care for their patients. All that remains of this immense complex today are the limestone foundation walls still supporting the hillside at the foot of the bluff.

THE ELMS RESORT & SPA

While many haunted locations have limited and often rustic accommodations, travelers to Excelsior Springs can stay in the lap of luxury at the Elms Resort & Spa, where the ghosts have been known to visit guests in their rooms while dining on an exquisite meal or even indulging in a luxurious massage. Listed in the National Register of Historic Places, the historic Elms is also a place where ghost-hunting equipment is welcome, and the staff happily takes the time to fill visitors in on their most recent otherworldly experiences.

It was my close friend Kate Fields who first told me of Excelsior Springs and the Elms. Her eyes were sparkling with excitement when she said, "You have *got* to see this place." She was well aware of my love of history and the paranormal, and knew I would be impressed with the mere sight of this incredible resort. She was absolutely correct. Just turning one's car south onto Elms Drive in Excelsior Springs will fill any ghost hunter's mind with possibilities, for the Elms, only a block away, dominates the landscape and sends a small shiver of excitement down the spine.

For me it was love at first sight. I fell for the Elms and, after just a few short visits, fell in love with the people and the rich history of Excelsior Springs. And—what would be an amazing find for any avid paranormal adventurer—I discovered a vast treasure trove of ghostly tales describing paranormal activity in the city.

The Elms began in the year 1888, a time when Jack the Ripper started his killing spree in London, the Washington Monument opened to the public, and George Eastman registered the trademark "Kodak," but it is still another 40 years before the accidental discovery of penicillin by Prof. Alexander Fleming. In this bygone era, Excelsior Springs with its miraculous healing waters began emerging onto the national scene as the latest and greatest cure-all destination and vacation resort town. In the midst of the hustle and bustle of tourism, the first incarnation of the Elms majestically arose.

In a town made famous for the restorative properties of the natural spring waters, the Elms hotel was placed strategically close to the site of the sulpho-saline well, which was already a popular tourist attraction. This grand resort was developed in the midst of a 50-acre park that featured lush, relaxing gardens surrounding the extensive three-story resort. The wood-frame

The first Elms hotel, captured in this 1890s view, was constructed in 1888 on 50 acres. It measured 300 feet by 176 feet and contained 200 guest rooms. The first two floors of the hotel featured wooden verandas that were 16 feet wide. (From the Missouri Valley Special Collections, Kansas City Public Library, Kansas City, Missouri.)

Listed in the National Register of Historic Places, the Elms hotel was placed near the site of the Sulpho-Saline Well, which drew visitors from around the world. As a major tourism destination for the town of Excelsior Springs, multiple postcards of the hotel were distributed in an effort to increase interest among the affluent health-minded travelers of the time. This view is dated around the 1890s. (From the private collection of Betty Bissell.)

building measured 300 feet by 176 feet and contained 200 guest rooms. The first and second floors had beautiful wraparound wooden verandas that were 16 feet wide.

Just 100 yards to the west of the hotel, guests could enjoy swimming in a 60-by-30-foot pool filled with water from the sulpho-saline well that was maintained at a constant 72 degrees. Next to the mineral water pool, guests at the Elms enjoyed a variety of amenities, which included a target range and a four-lane bowling alley. Perhaps the oldest ghost story originating in Excelsior Springs happened near the site of the original Elms bowling alley.

On Monday, October 22, 1906, the *Excelsior Springs Daily Call* printed a story titled simply, "A Ghost Scare." The small article explains that on Saturday night, several people were frightened by "an apparition which appeared near the old Elms bowling alley." Witnesses described the mysterious entity as being "eight feet tall, garbed in white, and very luminous." The article tells of men and boys setting out as a group to catch the ghost, only to run panic-stricken at the sight of it.

A somewhat similar article appeared in the local *Excelsior Springs Daily Standard* paper just two months earlier, on August 14, 1906. This time the story was titled, "Ghost Scare at Liberty." The description of the ghostly appearance in nearby Liberty was vastly different from the Excelsior Springs sighting. The Liberty ghost was described as being tall, wearing a long black cape and hood, having inch-long teeth, and being as black as the ace of spades. The description of this Liberty ghost is somewhat reminiscent of the Victorian-era character of Spring-Heeled Jack.

Beginning in the 1800s, descriptions of a frightening entity started popping up in London, Liverpool, and even Scotland. Dubbed "Spring-Heeled Jack" because he was reported to be able to take great leaps, he has been described as having a terrifying appearance and wearing a black cloak. Like the Liberty ghost, Spring-Heeled Jack was also reported as be tall and thin, having razor-sharp teeth, and sporting a black cloak.

Fire completely ravaged the first Elms hotel after just 10 years of operation during the early morning hours of May 8, 1898. Specific details on the blaze were provided by historian Harry Soltysiak in an article printed in the *Kansas City Star* on October 30, 1998. The fire began in the basement in the Elms bakery and quickly spread throughout the building. Fire crews were quickly dispatched but were sadly ineffectual due to the coupling on the fire hoses not fitting the hydrants near the Elms. Although the resort was completely destroyed, fortunately no one was injured or killed in the blaze.

It would be yet another 10 years before a second Elms hotel would be constructed at a cost of $225,000 by the Elms Realty Company of Kansas City. Construction began in 1908 on a location slightly to the south of the original structure. The first Elms lay along the area that now comprises Elms Boulevard and faced the Fishing River. Plans for the second Elms hotel included the building facing toward the downtown area. Construction efforts were slowed early on, when in June severe flooding in the area collapsed a stone wall on the eastern side of the building, forcing the masonry work to be redone at a cost of an additional $10,000. Unlike the wooden structure of the first hotel, the second Elms was built of sturdy and attractive native limestone and included 225 guest rooms. No formal ceremony was held when the second Elms opened its doors to its first guests on July 24, 1909.

The credit for the design of the new incarnation of the Elms is often given to the famous Kansas City architect Louis S. Curtiss, but there is some confusion in the matter. It is the same architect who just two years earlier, in 1906, crafted the Clay County State Bank. Additional information on the amazing architectural details and history of the bank building can be found in the chapter covering the Excelsior Springs Museum and Archives.

This confusion between architectural firms is understandable and continues to be a matter of debate. Frederick McIlvan was a longtime assistant of Louis Curtiss. In 1908, McIlvan left his employment with Curtiss and formed his own company in partnership with Frederick Hill.

Elms Hotel Ruins, 1910, Excelsior Springs, Mo.

Both the first Elms, which was constructed in 1888, and the second Elms, which was constructed in 1908, were destroyed by fire. This postcard clearly portrays the burned-out remains of the second Elms hotel, with its native limestone foundation and walls still partially standing. (From the Excelsior Springs Museum and Archives Collection, 1911.)

Dining Room, The New Elms, Excelsior Springs, Mo.

This 1911 postcard from the second Elms clearly reads, "Dining Room! The New Elms, Excelsior Springs, MO." The postmark on the back of this card is dated March 23, 1911. A handwritten note on the card states, "We did not put up at this hotel as it was burned up when we got here." (From the private collection of Jim Masson.)

On September 7, 1912, the third and final version of the Elms hotel was created in the Tudor Revival style; this postcard captures the hotel in 1919. The final version of the Elms stands one story taller than its predecessor and accommodates a larger number of guests. (From the private collection of Betty Bissell.)

This 1920s photograph includes a full frontal view of the third Elms hotel and a side view of the building. Constructed of native limestone with a steel frame and reinforced concrete, the third Elms included as many fire prevention tactics as possible at the time. The Elms hotel opened once again on September 7, 1912, with over 3,000 well-wishers on hand. (From the Missouri Valley Special Collections, Kansas City Public Library, Kansas City, Missouri.)

It was this new team of McIlvan and Hill who are credited with working on the project of the second Elms hotel.

In 1906, while Louis Curtiss was working on the designs for the Clay County State Bank, he was also working on the plans for the El Bisonte Hotel in Hutchinson, Kansas. The McIlvan and Hill plans for the second Elms are extremely comparable to the El Bisonte Hotel design. Many years later, after the passing of Curtiss, plans for the second Elms hotel were found among his affects. It may be possible that the initial work on the layout of the second Elms began in the offices of Curtiss and that McIlvan took the project with him when he left.

On October 30, 1910, in an odd twist of fate, this second Elms, like the first, burned to the ground. It was nearly 1:00 a.m. on a Sunday when the first signs of a fire coming from a shed near the kitchen were noticed. That night, there were over 140 guests in the Elms hotel, many of who had only recently settled in for the night after enjoying a Saturday night dance. Unlike the first fire that destroyed the Elms, the firemen quickly arrived and appeared to have some success in controlling the blaze.

Unfortunately, the fire began to spread inward and upward, forcing guests to flee from the smoke, and they were unable to retrieve their belongings. By 2:15 a.m., the building was completely aflame. A portion of the wall to the east collapsed, catching a fireman underneath the smoldering rubble. Other firemen quickly rushed to his aide and rescued him from the debris. Amazingly, once again, no one reported being harmed in the blaze.

After the complete destruction of the second Elms, efforts started with reviewing the damage, and salvage began with hopes of rebuilding once more. Incredibly, on November 3, 1910, the hotel safe was discovered under the ashen remains. Property of the hotel guests was found intact and undamaged. This fireproof safe can still be seen today at the top of the grand marble staircase. It is a silent testament to the fire that destroyed the second Elms over 100 years ago.

Once again, like a phoenix rising from the ashes, the Elms rose to reclaim its former glory. Wisely, the owners invested heavily in the new hotel, adding every feature known for the day to help deter a future fiery demise. The final and largest version of the Elms was created with native limestone taken in part from the second building, steel frames, and reinforced concrete. Created in the Tudor Revival style, the final version of the Elms stands one story taller than its predecessor to accommodate even greater numbers of visitors. On September 7, 1912, in full media hype and with a crowd of over 3,000 well-wishers, the grand Elms again opened its doors.

HAUNTED ROOMS

Room 140

A frequent traveler to the Elms is a man I will refer to as Mr. Waller, whose business often required he stay for extended periods of time. Since Room 140 has great access from the main floor areas and includes a nice layout with good work areas, Waller always requested it during his stays. At first, he was unaware of any ghostly resident in his room, but over time, he would begin to wake up in the night feeling as if someone was watching him. After searching the room on the first few visits, Waller became comfortable with his ghostly visitor and thought nothing of continuing to stay in Room 140. But on subsequent stays, it seems the ghost of Room 140 became more comfortable with Waller as well and began sitting on the end of the bed. These visits left a visible indention on the bedspread.

Mr. Waller was becoming increasingly uncomfortable, but he still enjoyed the layout and the location of the room and was not easily frightened by just a dent on the end of the bed, so he continued coming to the Elms again and again, staying in his favorite room. More time passed, and with additional visits to the Elms, once again Waller became relaxed with the extra "guest" in Room 140—that is, until the ghost began to exert his authority over the room and especially over the bed.

One night, Mr. Waller awoke to find his entire body being pushed down forcefully onto the mattress, and despite his best efforts he was unable for a period of time to overcome the invisible weight bearing down upon his chest. It was as if the ghost had simply forgotten Waller was in the room and had lain down in the bed to rest directly on top of the sleeping guest! That must have been the last straw, for although Waller still frequents the Elms on a regular basis, he refuses to stay in Room 140 ever again.

Room 140 was the spot for a thorough investigation conducted by team members from KCPI (Kansas City Paranormal Investigators) in the late fall of 2008. During their late-night stakeout of the ghost in this suite, one team member felt a brush on her arm, while another felt an uncomfortable presence near the end of the bed. Later, under close scrutiny of the sound recordings taking during the investigation, a very deep male voice can be heard whispering his desires to the female team members of KCPI.

An added note from the management: the ghost of Room 140 does not appear to be of a threatening or frightening nature. For those comfortable with a paranormal experience, this should be one of the first rooms to request for an overnight stay.

Room 438

Although no background evidence has yet to be uncovered about the ghost in Room 438, this room too should be on the list if one is requesting a haunted overnight stay. As further proof of the haunting, be certain to ask at the hotel check-in counter for a picture of the ghost of room 438.

In 2006, a young couple stayed at the Elms and took several photographs while staying in room 438. It was several days later, after they had returned home, that they discovered something very unusual about one of their photographs; an extra person can clearly be seen in the picture. Since the Elms does not have the original photograph in their possession, a thorough examination to rule out any tampering or camera error cannot be conducted. So, it is up to visitors to look the picture over and decide for themselves if indeed it is the genuine article.

On my first overnight stay at the Elms, it was a very good friend of mine, Kate, who volunteered to stay alone in Room 438 while I stayed with my paranormal team PEDRO (Paranormal Encounter Documentation and Research Organization) just a few rooms down the hall. Her personal experience is a testament to just how quickly the ghosts of the Elms can make their presence known. Since a paranormal investigation was planned for the evening, Kate spent the afternoon napping in the room in order to be alert for the late night of ghost hunting ahead.

She had difficulty dropping off to sleep. There was a constant sound of water running coming from the bathroom. In her drowsy state, Kate had passed this sound off as possibly an overactive flushing system, but the sound kept waking her up. Finally, she got up and went into the restroom to jiggle the handle on the toilet, only to discover that the sound was produced by water in the faucet running at full speed. Later, when discussing this incident, Kate showed our team just how difficult it is to lift the handle on the faucet. It takes a good strong upward pull, which ruled out the possibility of high water pressure lifting the handle, especially when taking into consideration that we were up on the fourth floor.

The team did an investigation of the room with little results. Many photographs were taken in an attempt to reproduce the ghostly photograph presented in the lobby. From different angles, lights, and camera settings, the team was not able to physically reproduce the ghostly face that had appeared on the picture they had seen. The only surprising evidence was a series of small orbs that appeared in every picture under different lighting conditions and from several angles.

VIEW OF PARK
~ ELMS HOTEL ~
Excelsior Springs,
Mo.

This 1930s postcard features guests relaxing on the grounds behind the Elms hotel. This area has been renovated over the years and currently contains an outdoor swimming pool, hot tub, and wooden gazebo for outdoor events. (From the private collection of Betty Bissell.)

For many years, it was believed that this 1940s family photograph of Virginia Maxine (Cain) Hightower had been taken on the grounds of the Elms. Recent research has discovered that the image was actually taken on the grounds of the nearby Veterans Administration Hospital. Both Excelsior Springs locations featured extensive, beautifully manicured grounds. (From the private collection of Brenda [Hightower] Berger.)

These orbs were always in the same location, in the same spot as the appearance of the apparition in the photograph taken in the room.

When management at the hotel was asked to comment of the occurrence of the water turning itself on in the sink, they were amazed. Although it might be expected to discover leaky pipes and disparate level of water pressure in an older building such as the Elms, the hotel had been completely replumbed during renovations in the late 1990s. Management also testified that there had been no other reports by hotel guests of the water faucets turning on by themselves in Room 438.

Room 300, the Truman Suite

Room 300 at the Elms is easy to find. One can take the grand staircase past the Truman Boardroom and the Library Lounge and continue a few short steps to the third floor. Take the west wing, pass the Capone Suite, and hang a left at the end of the hallway. Room 300 proudly bares an oval plaque beside the door designating it as "The Truman Suite."

It was election night on November 2, 1948, and the 34th president of the United States and some of his secret service agents were welcome guests at the Elms. Pres. Harry S. Truman had been a frequent visitor in the past. He knew the Elms and its staff were well equipped to provide for the needs of these special guests. The decision to spend the night on this special occasion was also due in part to the location of the hotel in Excelsior Springs, for it was over 30 miles away from the pressures of the Democratic National Headquarters in nearby Kansas City. The Elms was also chosen because it was the perfect place to unwind at the end of a long campaign trail that had taken the president and his group across 30,000 miles by rail on his historic whistle-stop campaign tour.

Rated the underdog by national media, Truman took a break from his busy day and the mounting pressure to enjoy several relaxing spa treatments offered at the hotel. The president then returned to join his staff in what is now Room 300 to listen to the election returns on the radio. When all the votes were tallied, President Truman amazingly defeated his nearest opponent, Republican candidate Thomas Dewey, by winning 56 percent of the electoral vote.

Staying in the Truman Suite can help take one's imagination back to the heyday of Excelsior Springs and the healing-water resorts. The room has been respectfully decorated with pictures, articles, and books on Pres. Harry S. Truman. Upon entering this extensive suite, guests can sense the atmosphere that almost sizzles with the excitement Truman himself must have felt when he discovered that against all odds and popular belief he had retained the highest office in the land.

This amazing turn of events put the Elms in the media spotlight of the day. Owners of the hotel realized the value in helping spread the word of their famous guest and this fateful evening. Two years later, they were still attempting to capitalize on the story when they took out a rather good-sized ad in the *Chicago Tribune* on December 3, 1950, reading in very large type, "ON ELECTION DAY The-Man-Who-Didn't-Have-a-Chance enjoyed a Magic Mineral Water Bath and MIRACLE MASSAGE at the famous ELMS HOTEL EXCELSIOR SPRINGS YOU KNOW WHAT HAPPENED! You too, can improve your luck Looks and *lifeline* with a sojourn at America's No. 1 Spa-Resort." A smaller caption near the bottom reads, "100% fireproof."

In mid-November 2008, the PEDRO team spent the night in this room only a few days after the historic election of America's first African American president, Barack Obama. While team members were busy investigating other haunted areas in the rest of the spacious resort in the middle of the night, they left a camcorder recording in the darkened bedroom. During more than two hours of the recordings, several short segments captured a small light dancing across the room. The elevation of the room eliminates a great deal of possible interference from outside, such as car lights reflecting across the room. These results justify further investigation of this history-making suite.

Yesterday upon the Stair, Jamie J. Fanning, and the Witching Hour

Popular folklore maintains that the Witching Hour is a time when supernatural beings are thought to be at their most powerful, the time of night when ghosts may effortlessly manifest themselves. This hour is typically midnight or any time within the period from midnight to 3:00 a.m. Shakespeare refers to this period during a soliloquy from *Hamlet* (3.2.380–384): "Tis now the very witching time of night, / When churchyards yawn and hell itself breathes out / Contagion to this world: now could I drink hot blood, / And do such bitter business as the day / Would quake to look on."

Perhaps it is because of the Witching Hour that Jamie Fanning (better known to his friends and coworkers as "Jay"), night engineer of the Elms Resort & Spa, has reported far more personal paranormal experiences than his coworkers. Or perhaps it is simply that his duties take him far away from the noises of daytime resort activities and away from areas of the hotel guests to locations of total seclusion and utter silence, where all explanations other than the paranormal can be quickly ruled out.

The Main Stairway

The winding stairway between floors on the south side of the resort is a well-traveled route for many hotel guests. A quick walk down these stairs will bring one to the Library Lounge, the Truman Board Room, and then on down into the hotel lobby. While walking down the stairs, there is a terrific panoramic view of the outside pool area, the gazebo, and the wooded grounds. Even at night, it would be difficult not to pause for a moment and take in the spectacular view.

On this particular night, Jay was taking a quick glance out the window while coming down the staircase. His progress had taken him only as far as the landing between the fourth and third floors. Peering out the window at night created a clear reflection on the glass of the staircase behind him. During this stop, Jay managed to spy a little more than just the outside grounds. His eye easily caught the reflection of a well-shaped pair of female legs coming down the stairs behind him. He noticed she was wearing a pair of black high heels with little bows on the top of each shoe. Then, upon hearing the soft rustle of fabric, Jay looked even closer at the reflection to see a very short black skirt.

Hotel staff must never appear to be rude, and so rather than be caught noticing her shapely legs in a reflection, he quickly turned around, asking, "How are you enjoying your stay?" His words met with empty air as Jay discovered he was alone on the staircase. It would have been impossible for her to have passed by without his noticing. Tread gently as you take in the view from the main staircase between floors at the Elms, or you might never find out if the sound of footsteps behind you are of human or ghostly origin.

The Lap-Pool Stairway

There have been other incidents upon the stairs, but one of the most memorable occasions for Jay was late one night on the staircase from the spa area down to the level with the lap pool.

The marble staircase is located between the lobby and the Library Lounge. A dark shadow has been seen silently gliding down these stairs. The fireproof safe retrieved from the ruins of the second Elms hotel can be seen perched on the landing above. (Author's collection.)

This staircase is on the east side of the hotel. Jay had already locked the outside doors for the night to insure no hotel guests crept down for a late-night swim. As always, the doors are locked exactly at midnight to allow him time for a few maintenance duties in this subterranean area of the hotel.

Just as Jay was opening the safety gate at the top of the staircase, he caught a wisp of smoke in the reflection of the glass surrounding the staircase. Double-checking behind him for visitors has become a full-time duty, and Jay quickly checked the landing to be certain no one else was around and to see that there was no fire or smoke lingering in the air. But there once again was a quick wisp of smoke reflected only in the glass at the far side of the staircase. Then the smoky reflection grew and became quite large. The massy haze moved across from one windowpane to the next, inching closer and closer all the while. At last, the smoke in the reflection was only on the glass of the outside door. Then, as quickly as it had appeared, the smoky reflection in the glass vanished. No reasonable explanation has been found for the mysterious fog, nor has it appeared again.

The Marble Staircase

One final notable stairway haunting is the grand marble staircase between the lobby and the Library Lounge. Once again, in the middle of the night it was Jay who had an encounter with the other realm. He was standing near the check-in desk of the hotel lobby and caught a dark shadow coming down the stairs. At first, he paid little attention to the shadowy figure, mistaking it for a guest coming down to the lobby perhaps to purchase a late-night snack.

Jay briefly saw the upper torso of what he assumed was a man as it rounded the corner from the staircase between floors to come down the main marble staircase. Then the darkened apparition really caught his attention. It was solid black and was floating right next to the railing, actually against the rail and the wall. Most mysterious of all was the fact that this apparition had no head, arms, or feet, just a black shadowy torso floating in the air. The torso figure slid down the wall beside the staircase and continued to slide down and around to another staircase leading to the floor below. Without a moment's hesitation—for now Jay had become quite familiar with such encounters—he quickly crossed the lobby and rushed down the stairs to the lower level. He wasn't too surprised to find there were no humans and no ghosts waiting for him at the foot of the stairs. Whatever presence had slipped quietly down the stairs, it had also slipped back into the realm from whence it came.

A quick note for all researchers and historians: the staircases at the Elms are generally either made of marble or steel. These materials were chosen during the construction of the third and current location as a deterrent to fire, which destroyed the first two Elms hotels.

Ghost on the Elevator

The guest elevator at the Elms Resort & Spa is small and cozy, but at the Elms even small spaces can harbor their own spirits. One of the first sightings of the elevator ghost came during a time when the hotel was closed for renovations in the early 1980s, and thus there was obviously no staff. The new owner was staying on to oversee improvements to the building. Few other people were allowed in the hotel, just construction workers, and they had already gone home for the evening.

The owner was in the lobby with her dog at her side. She watched in rapt attention as she heard the elevator come to the main floor and the doors open. She thought that there must be an intruder in the building or a workman leaving behind schedule. Strangely enough, she could also hear a long, low growl emanating from her pet.

EXCELSIOR SPRINGS: HAUNTED HAVEN

A woman dressed in a maid's uniform stepped forth from the elevator. Her uniform did not fit the apparel of the time but seemed more fitting to the 1920s or 1930s uniforms of the Elms staff. Not only did the owner watch as she moved off the elevator, but her dog reacted too. Together they observed the maid walk just a few steps forward and then simply vanish into thin air.

During a large-scale investigation of the Elms in November 2008, it was well past 2:00 a.m. when Kansas City Paranormal Investigators packed several members of their team onto the Elms elevator with strict orders for silence. While the group squeezed in tightly with a large amount of equipment, they smiled at each other but held to their vow of silence. Later, upon reviewing the digital recordings taken during this silent ride, a woman's voice is heard clearly asking, "Can I leave now?" Did Kansas City Paranormal Investigators have an encounter with the ghostly maid on the elevator? The team is planning to return for further investigation of this haunted area of the Elms and yet another late-night elevator ride.

HAUNTED SPACES

Truman Board Room

Guests signing in at the front desk of the Elms need only look up to see the windows of the Truman Board Room. This private meeting room is the only room at the Elms with windows facing towards the inside of the building. When peering down from the inside of the boardroom, it is easy to view the front entrance doors and the main floor of the lobby. Since there was absolutely no possibility of policemen sneaking up on players in this room with a view, it became the location for high-stakes poker games during the 1920s and 1930s.

Infamous Al Capone himself is rumored to have played a few hands of poker in the Truman Board Room during his visits to the Elms. Capone was a Prohibition-era gangster and leader of a crime syndicate involved in illegal activities, including smuggling, bootlegging, and racketeering. He always traveled with a well-armed entourage of bodyguards.

During the late 1990s, Brenda, the human resources manager for the Elms, was leaving for day. She was standing at the front desk in the lobby and by chance found herself peering up at the windows to the Truman Board Room. Something was moving in the room, and it caught her eye. This movement concerned her greatly, for the room had already been locked up tightly for the night. What she saw next was astounding, for she found herself looking directly up the barrel of a tommy gun pointed right at her! It was only for a moment, and then the image disappeared into thin air.

Other paranormal experiences in this room have included the sounds of clinking glasses heard outside the doorway, the smell of cigar smoke lingering in the air, and the unmistakable sounds of men arguing over a game of cards.

During an initial visit to the Elms, the PEDRO investigative team spent a considerable amount of time in the Truman Board Room. Temperature readings taken in various locations gleaned surprising results, as a significant cold spot seemed to move from chair to chair. The chairs were next to the outside windows, so possibly the unusually cold readings were due to a draft from the cool outside air. Then, just a few minutes later, a team member felt a hand brush against her back. The PEDRO team feels this area of the Elms requires additional investigation as a potential hot spot for paranormal activity.

Indoor Lap-Pool Area

After descending a flight of stairs to the indoor lap-pool area, visitors will immediately notice the increase in humidity and the rise in temperature due in part to the hot tub at the far end of the

The water in the lap pool is maintained at a constant 72-degree temperature. Unusual sounds have been reported in this area. Some noises may be residual hauntings from the days when the room was a 1920s speakeasy where a murder took place. (Author's collection.)

room. The water in the extensive lap pool is maintained at a constant 72-degree temperature, making it the ideal environment for swimming. This room has also become the ideal environment for ghostly activities, including several different types of paranormal haunting phenomena that have been reported in the area.

The most frequently reported disturbances on this floor are unusual sounds such as loud bangs, scrapping noises, and soft murmurs. Although some of these sounds may be attributed to the machinery of the pumps for the lap pool, cool tub, and hot tub, other sounds may in fact be residual haunting sounds from the days when the entire room was not a pool area but a 1920s speakeasy.

A murder did take place in this room during its days as a speakeasy. A gentleman was shot and killed over a game of cards. It is not difficult to assume that other ghostly sounds, such as gunshots followed by a woman's screams, occasionally reported in this area by guests and staff of the Elms could also be linked to this gruesome killing. This too may be the explanation of the uneasy feeling described by those unlucky travelers lingering just a little too long in the doorway between the pool area and the workout room.

Three full-bodied ghosts have also been seen in and around the lap pool. The ghost seen most frequently is the apparition of a little boy swimming in the water. This can be very surprising for hotel guests who are unaware the child is a spirit. These unsuspecting guests often rush up to hotel staff voicing concern for a child left alone in the water without parental supervision. Sadly, there was an actual drowning of an eight-year-old boy a few decades ago, which most people have attributed to this haunting little figure.

I was fortunate enough to investigate the lap-pool area around 1:00 a.m. in November 2008 with the paranormal investigation team PAI (Paranormal Activity Investigators). PAI has a unique and successful style of ghost hunting that sets their team apart from others. PAI investigations are often loud and full of fun. As Becky Ray (one of the teams founding members) puts it, "Ghosts are just like people, they want to go where it looks like everyone is having fun. They like to drop in and share in a good time." Their method was quickly proven when I personally saw a team member cry out to the boy spirit known to haunt the pool area to "get out of the water quick!"

Amazingly, a strong straight line in the otherwise empty water came directly towards us against the current. I hopped up and tried to capture the event on film, but by the time I reached the pool's edge the movement in the water had stopped. Everyone participating was visibly moved and tried again and again to see something happening in the water, but only small swirls from the current could be seen. Then a small squeal was heard from the opposite side of the pool. A female team member had stumbled upon small, child-sized watery footprints leading away from the pool. The footprints started out as a small puddle at the poolside and then lasted but four brief steps in the opposite direction from where the team had been attempting to contact the child.

Another ghost of the lap pool area was witnessed by Jay, the night engineer at the Elms. This ghost too was seen as a full-bodied apparition. The encounter with this specter was rare indeed, for as Jay was about to leave the pool area to return upstairs he spotted a man sitting in one of the chaise lounges just a short distance from the doorway. Undoubtedly due to his vast experience with the ghosts of the Elms, Jay knew instinctively that this visage seated in the chair was a phantom and not a living being. But what transpired next is only reported in an exceptional few number of paranormal cases. The ghost leaned slightly forward, titled his head to the side, and followed Jay's movements as he headed towards the stairs. It was as if the ghost was not only fully aware of Jay's presence but also wanted Jay to be aware he was being watched. Without further confrontation, Jay boldly went on his way up the stairs and back to work.

The Grand Ballroom

For nearly a century, the Grand Ballroom at the Elms has been hosting one memorable event after another. From breakfasts to luncheons to dinners and late-night dances, this room is often utilized by many different groups during the same day. As the largest rental space at the Elms, the area has been the social headquarters for large gatherings from Excelsior Springs and beyond, acting as host to high school and college reunions, family reunions, and large wedding receptions. It would be impossible to count the number of meetings and meals hosted by community groups in this room over the years, which may be why the parties and meeting sounds linger on well after the tables and chairs have been placed aside and the lights have been turned off for the night.

A repeating phenomenon for this room is, oddly enough, the sounds of opera singing. This otherworldly vocal performance has been reported by several members of the staff, including Nicki, a former housekeeper at the Elms. No one interviewed offered a possible source or paranormal basis for the opera singing. Research has shown that the historic Music Hall once stood well within hearing distance of the first Elms. At times in 1898, the Music Hall and the Elms served as extensions of each other when convention services were required. The Music Hall held over 1,300 patrons, and the seats could also be removed for meeting space or ballroom dancing. Guests at the Elms could open their windows or sit on the massive porches and enjoy the music lofting through the night air.

Nicki also confided that late one evening, while she was cleaning up after yet another large event, a vacuum cleaner plugged into the wall at the far side of the room turned on completely by itself.

Dangling from the ceiling of the Grand Ballroom are several large, ornate chandeliers. On many occasions, the chandelier at the south end of the room has been spotted swinging back and forth or noticeably shaking. During an investigation with Kansas City Paranormal Investigators, team member Dayna remarked that the shaking might be attributed to movement from people walking around in the Library Lounge above and the vibrations traveling up the beam. The team members were later very surprised to hear clearly on the digital voice recording taken during this time a second voice, from a disembodied entity, repeating the words immediately after her saying, "Up the beam."

Library Lounge Ghost

Linger for a late-night drink at the Library Lounge to hear the firsthand stories of the "Man in White" from bartender Pamela. One may have to wait until after midnight, when the drinkers have dwindled down to just a handful of guests, in order to gain her attention long enough for her to relate the eerie details. Then again, while waiting, one just might spy the Man in White himself, for he has been noticed by a great number of guests of the Elms.

Many thought for years that the Man in White was the ghost of an Elvis impersonator, Terry Tigre, who stayed frequently at the Elms while performing his act during the 1970s at the nearby Crestview Inn. Frequently a man in a bright white suit is seen walking through the Library Lounge and then disappearing into the wall. Up until recently, many believed that "Elvis" committed suicide at the Elms by leaping from a third-floor fire escape, and thus an urban legend was created, but a little research revealed a couple of astonishing twists to this tale.

As it turns out, it was not the impersonator but his booking manager who died from the fall at the Elms. There was some speculation that he had been drinking, but no one at the time felt it was a suicide, since the booking manager was happily married with four small children waiting for his return. The little information that is known about this untimely death was reported in

When the lounge is closed for the evening, the outside doors are securely locked. One morning, when the doors were unlocked by the bartender, all of the bar's drinking glasses were lined up single file from the doorway all the way to the bar. Behind locked doors, every single glass had been placed in a row, creating an unforgettable display. (Author's collection.)

The son of Jesse James became a lifesaver for his mother and sister after his father was killed. Jesse Edwards James worked and paid for their home and his sister Susan's education while getting a law degree for himself. This image was probably taken around the time of the 1902 exhumation of the remains of Jesse James, which he attended. (From the Ellison Collection.)

the Excelsior Springs newspaper, the *Daily Standard*, on Monday, October 23, 1978. According to newspaper accounts, it was late, the room was overheated due to a broken air-conditioning unit, and the man simply stepped out onto the fire escape for a breath of fresh air—unfortunately his last!

It may be the voice of the booking agent that PEDRO investigator Joe Kline heard late one night during an investigation of the Library Lounge: "It happened late one night when three of us were seated at a table near the window holding an interview session with the ghost. We were the only living souls in the bar at the time. From behind, a disembodied voice whispered in my ear, 'It's time to go on now.' " Joe Kline speculates that this may have been the voice of the booking manager still working with his client; the Elvis impersonator also died in an automobile accident several years later. So just who is this mysterious Man in White? It may never be known whether it is the ghost of the lingering lounge lizard or his booking manager—or perhaps the two are still touring their show together in the other realm.

The Man in White has been spotted on many occasions sitting in a chair at the end of the bar, hanging out near the piano and staring out the window. Pamela once spotted someone watching her from the windows inside of the Library Lounge while she was relaxing in the hot tub outside. After her swim, she stopped to check with Jay Fanning to find out who had dared to enter the bar against regulations and prior to business hours. They both went to check the room, only to discover the doors were still tightly locked. No living person could have entered the room.

Additional stories surrounding the mysterious Man in White, as well as other eerie spirits of the Elms Resort & Spa, can be found in *Haunted Missouri* by Jason Offutt and *Ghost in the Mirror* by Leslie Rule.

Pamela does not frighten easily, and she was accustomed to catching a glimpse of the lingering lounge lizard from time to time, but one event has kept her from ever again entering or working in the Library Lounge alone. After the lounge is closed for the evening, the outside doors are securely locked, and the key is placed downstairs inside of a locked cabinet. Arriving to work one day, she obtained the key to the room. When Pamela unlocked the doors, she discovered an amazing sight—many of the books along the western wall had been pushed around on the shelves, and most of them were now lying on their sides. Even more incredible to behold was the sight of drinking glasses, single file in a straight line, all the way across the floor between the open door leading to the bar. Mysteriously, behind locked doors, every single glass from within the bar had been removed from the shelves and placed in a row, creating an unforgettable display.

Adding to the tales of intrigue surrounding Excelsior Springs and the Elms during this time, while local papers were reporting the death of the faux Elvis's manager, the national stage was focusing on the exhumation of Jesse James's remains at the James Farm Museum in nearby Kearney, Missouri. James's remains were exhumed by scientists for DNA analysis to determine if, in fact, they were from the actual body of Jesse James. Speculation as to who was actually buried in the quiet grave in 1882, Jesse James or a mistaken imposter, began almost as quickly as the original burial took place. The story of the Terry Tigre show agent and the exhumation of Jesse James remains shared the front page of the *Excelsior Springs Standard* on that fateful day. Later it was reported that it was indeed Jesse James who had been interred at the family farm. The DNA matched at 99.79 percent.

Ghostly Activity in the Lobby

The lobby of the Elms is one of the most timeless locations inside the resort. Although some features of the area have changed slightly during its nearly 100 years of service to the public, the ornate marble floors, high-beamed ceiling, and large stone fireplace are the perfect setting to the beginning of a relaxing, peaceful vacation.

Sometimes in paranormal investigations, one learns to ask the right questions, and at other times plain old-fashioned persistence and luck can pay off as well. When I first asked Alicia, a night clerk at the front desk of the Elms, if she had ever seen a ghost while she was working, her answer was a direct but polite "no." Not letting myself get too discouraged, I later returned to the front desk when other guests were not around and rephrased my question: "Have you ever had anything unusual happen while working at the Elms?" This time, Alicia was a wealth of information, as she began to relate the following tales.

The first time something unusual occurred during her evening shift was on a rather ordinary night. Guests had for the most part settled in for the evening, and it was time to start sorting through the necessary paperwork portion of her job. There was a fairly large pile of papers stacked next to her workstation, and Alicia was busy entering information on the front-desk computer. Almost as if an unseen person was playing a practical joke, one by one the papers began to cascade down onto the floor. If Alicia had accidentally bumped into the stack, the papers would have tumbled down all at once. Rather than being amused, the night clerk found the situation fairly frustrating, since the tumbled paperwork resulted in considerably more time to complete her tasks.

The next otherworldly incident once occurred again on a typical business evening after most of the hotel guests had left the lobby area for the night. Alicia had just taken notice of an empty drinking glass left in the center of the east side of the wide glass counter of the registration desk, and she assumed that it was most likely left behind by a late-night guest from the downstairs bar. She turned her back for just a moment, busy with the never-ending paperwork required of her position. She looked at the empty glass again to find it still in its original position on the countertop, but the glass was completely shattered. Alicia was never aware of the sound of anyone approaching, nor did she hear what should have been the sounds of glass breaking only a few feet from where she stood.

She had one last tale to relate to which had occurred just a week earlier, while the entire PEDRO team was busy on-site conducting a paranormal investigation of the lap-pool area on a lower level. The inner glass doors of the lobby flew all the way open as if a guest had walked in quickly and just pushed them aside, but there was no one in the area. This event was also witnessed by Nicki, another staff member who was busy cleaning the floor in the lobby. The two women rushed to each other to discuss the situation. Desperately they tried to find a natural cause for the event that had just unfolded before their eyes. Sometimes the doors move slightly due to wind coming in from the other entrance doors to the west, but this late at night, the western lobby access doors were locked. They even ruled out wind from the north, since neither employee had witnessed movement from the outer pair of glass doors.

The Haunted Spa at the Elms

While walking into the entrance of the spa at the Elms, guests can view several historical photographs of some of the natural springs that led to the growth of the Excelsior Springs area. This brief hallway entrance also serves as a well-placed transitional space from the hotel proper into the luxurious elegance of the spa within. Immediately the eye is drawn to a smiling face behind the service counter. Scattered about the room are items for purchase to enhance the experience of a stay at the Elms, from bathing suits to jewelry to spa-quality hair products. It can be difficult to pass this area without stopping to shop.

During the most recent renovations to the Elms, expansions were made to the original spa at the Elms, including an upper level consisting of a therapy section with four private rooms. It was not long after reopening this renovated section of the resort that yet another ghost made its presence known.

Amanda was a new massage therapist for the spa at the Elms and was in the middle of a busy day, and yet she was also doing her best to create an atmosphere of peaceful relaxation for a guest while giving a European massage. Relaxing music was playing, the soft aroma of incense was wafting in the air, and the lights were dimmed. There was nothing about the day, the setting, or the general mood of the room to prepare her or the unsuspecting Elms guest for what was about to occur. From across the room, a clock flew directly off the wall. It came straight forward about five feet through the air to hit her directly across the shoulders. Close examination of the clock, the wall, and the area did not result in any natural explanation for this strange occurrence.

A little shaken but still enjoying her employment with the spa at the Elms, Amanda decided to move future spa clientele in her care to the massage therapy room directly across the hall from the room where the disturbing incident took place. Just a few days later, the ghost once again found an object to throw at the unsuspecting Amanda. Fortunately, this time the specter chose a much softer object—a tissue box that was sitting only inches away on a countertop propelled itself into the air and hit her squarely on the backside.

The term "poltergeist" is most commonly used for paranormal activities where objects fly and items are thrown at unsuspecting people in the vicinity. In his book *The Ghost Hunters Guidebook*, Troy Taylor included the following description this paranormal occurrence:

> Poltergeist: the word literally means, "noisy ghost" in German. Although it actually refers to traditional ghosts and hauntings, in other cases, it can be used to describe the work of a human agent. In this situation, the knockings and the movements of objects is caused by an outward explosion on kinetic energy from the human mind. Most poltergeist outbreaks are short-lived.

The majority of documented poltergeist cases have centered near the presence of young adults during their preteen and teenage years. These events are frequently short term in nature. While no adolescents were near the spa to tie to these poltergeist–like events, fortunately for the staff members involved, they were short-term in nature and no additional ghostly events have been reported for several years.

Behind-the-Scenes Ghosts

Another Elms bartender, Pam, has experienced a few unexplained occurrences of her own. Her duties as the bartender of the beautifully restored historic bar just off the lobby have placed her alone in isolated areas late at night. It was a dark night, and after the bar was closed Pam was busy as usual clearing and cleaning the antique bar. She was preparing to rinse off a few items in the small recessed sink when the water turned on mysteriously all by itself. This problem was easily solved with a quick turn of the handle.

Not so easily solved was the night Pam was working in the kitchen behind the restaurant area. She was preparing glasses from the bar for the dishwasher by rinsing them in the sink, when inexplicably the water hose burst and the water gushed forth, drenching her from head to toe. As with the earlier story of water faucets turning on in room 438, a logical explanation could be that the water pressure at the Elms is a little high, but the entire building was replumbed during renovations in the late 1990s. Running water is often present in stories of paranormal encounters, and some believe it may act as a conduit or channel for a spirit to manifest. Ghostly or not, these incidents require closer examination.

Excelsior Springs: Haunted Haven

Haunted Objects at the Elms

Can spirits become attached to objects? Can ghosts hold on dearly to familiar items related to their lives or even possibly an object tied to the reason for their passing from this world into the next? Will moving this paranormally attached object from one room to the next, from one building to the next, even one city to the next somehow end its involvement with the other side? Or will the ghost simply move along with the object, following it to a new home, haunting a new vicinity?

It is with these questions in mind that I introduce two objects that are located within the present-day Elms that were resurrected from the previous Elms after that second devastating fire on October 30, 1910.

The Hotel Safe

Standing at the top of the marble staircase halfway between the lobby and the Library Lounge is a rather worn, beaten, faded black safe. It stands just over three feet high and is at least two feet wide. Large dials and strong hinges are on its fire-scarred door. Yet standing quietly in this tucked-away corner, this possibly haunted object can be easily overlooked.

A conversation with Megan, a long-term employee at the Elms, helped to point a finger in the direction of this antique safe as the possible epicenter of paranormal episodes occurring on and near the marble staircase, for twice Megan had seen something unusual on the stairs. Her current position at the Elms places her for long periods of time greeting guests and handling paperwork at the front business counter in the lobby, giving her an excellent vantage point to observe the following events.

Megan described her experience clearly, saying, "I saw a bright light out of the corner of my eye. It was near the top of the stairs, so high up that I had to bend over the counter to see it. I caught a glimpse of a glowing reddish orange bright light, but by the time I leaned over the counter to focus on it, the light was gone." Could it be just a mere coincidence or could the imprint of the devastating blaze of the past somehow be trapped within the aura of the safe?

Megan has also seen a shadowy figure descending the stairs. Her description of this apparition very closely matched the description by Jay of a similar shadow slipping down the marble staircase and vanishing down the wall. Perhaps the safe, seated silently at the top of the staircase, is why so many astounding ghost stories center around this area of the hotel.

The Furnace Boilerplate

On a lower level of the Elms, mounted directly into the wall, is the boilerplate retrieved from the former hotel. As with the safe, it too was rescued from beneath the debris of the fire. The boiler plate sticks out prominently from the wall. Some legends report guests hearing a loud knocking sounds emanating from behind the plate as if someone was on the other side knocking to get out, but I have yet to discover a first-hand report of the knocking sounds.

It was Megan who once again reported the ghostly activity in the area around the boilerplate. This story was actually given to Megan by her own brother Cameron, who also works at the Elms. It was very early one morning when Cameron arrived to meet with another employee before starting their shift. They were sitting and talking in the lower level at tables next to the place where the boilerplate is mounted on the wall. As Cameron was leaving to start his day, a shadowy figure caught his eye. He turned around and watched this figure of a man slowly walk as if drifting down the hall. Then the ghost turned sharply and walked directly into the boilerplate, vanishing completely and leaving behind only a very shocked and confused Elms employee.

Although the Elms Resort & Spa welcomes the occasional ghost-hunting team, it is best to call well in advance, inform the staff of one's intentions, and work within any and all guidelines

On the lower level, mounted into the wall, is the boilerplate retrieved from the second Elms hotel. It too was rescued from beneath the debris of the fire that destroyed the building. Local legends of loud knocking sounds emanating from behind the plate have been circulating for years. (Author's collection.)

requested. Investigators' respect for the staff and the property will help ensure the Elms is available for ghost hunters well into the future.

On the Grounds

The Gazebo and Carriage House

The grounds behind the Elms are ripe with the possibility of paranormal phenomena. Here on the extensive grounds are two additional structures. The first structure is the gazebo, which can easily be seen directly behind the building. This beautiful gazebo can hold up to 60 guests and has been the perfect spot for countless couples to take their wedding vows. Often the gazebo has played host to several wedding parties within the same day. If one takes a stroll late at night and stands beneath this large wooden-beamed structure, he or she can almost imagine the haunting images of former guests lounging about the lawns and dancing beneath the twinkling stars. One can feel their presence and wonder what future investigations may find.

The second structure is the carriage house. This building has been renovated to host smaller private parties and can be found further to the west of the property, across the street from the haunted Wabash BBQ. The PEDRO team has investigated this location on two separate occasions. While researching in advance about findings from other paranormal teams on carriage houses across the country, the team investigated with hopes of hearing the sounds of horses neighing or of the ringing of carriage bells.

What occurred in August 2008 has yet to be fully explained. Here, paranormal investigator Joe Kline reports his personal run-in with a fleeing "spirit in white":

It was nearing dusk and three members of the PEDRO team were in the carriage house meeting with a pair of team members from KCPI. We were seated together at one of the round tables while both teams were sharing and reviewing EVP files pulled from an investigation at the Elms earlier in the year. I was wearing headphones and listening to an EVP pulled from Room 140 when it appeared as though someone quickly ran by the back patio door of the carriage house. I clearly saw a man in white clothes silently run past and peer in at us through the glass of the door. The man's appearance was solid enough that I wasn't even considering that he could be a spirit; it had to be a person. I jumped up and ran out to the patio only to find there was no one in sight.

Upon further investigation we found that even the lightest steps clunked loudly on the wood deck and could be easily heard from the inside. So, it would have been impossible for a normal person to run across the deck without making a loud commotion. Additionally, the direction the image was running when he passed by the door would have taken him straight to the surrounding ravine that had an extremely sharp and dangerous drop-off. We stood as a group staring into the deep abyss wondering what had become of the man in white.

To those readers who are longing for even more ghostly tales of the Elms, I suggest further information can be found in *Haunted Missouri, A Ghostly Guide to the Show-Me State's Most Spirited Spots* by Jason Offutt.

The Elms Resort & Spa
401 Regent Street
Excelsior Springs, MO 64024
Phone: 1-800-THE ELMS or (816) 630-5500
www.elmsresort.com

THE ROYAL HOTEL

Sprawling, historic, abandoned, and haunted are just a few of the words that can be used when describing the Royal Hotel, located in the downtown district of Excelsior Springs, Missouri.

During the boom years of the city, when every home, boardinghouse, and hotel was literally overflowing with chronically ill guests, the Royal Hotel began its story. The doors first opened to the public in 1898 as Wholf's Tavern, the same year the first incarnation of the Elms hotel burned to the ground. Wholf's Tavern was renamed several times over the coming years. With a series of new owners and continual additions, the name changed from Wholf's Tavern to Grapple Tavern, then to Snapp Tavern, and then to the Hotel Royal, which later became better known as the Royal Hotel.

Between 1905 and 1910, the original hotel more than doubled in size with the addition of a six-story brick building directly to the west. This new dual-complex hotel hosted several commercial ventures on the first floor of the new building, including doctors' offices, a billiard parlor, a beauty parlor/barbershop, a jeweler, a cigar shop, and a café. The Royal Hotel also offered dancing in the Grand Ballroom to the Royal Hotel Orchestra, served up fine meals at the Royal Grill, and featured a sixth-floor Garden Room.

As with all other major locations in the early years of Excelsior Springs, the Royal Hotel came complete with its own source of mineral water; "Royal" salt sulfur water was served hot or cold in the hotel lobby, free of charge to hotel guests. Hotel guests could also visit the Royal Hotel Bath House for healing mineral water treatments and massage therapy complete with separate treatment areas for the men and the women.

From the 1980s until the final closing of the Royal Hotel in the late 1990s, the property was divided between 40 apartments and 45 hotel rooms. The building was badly in need of repair after nearly 100 years of service. A new owner replaced wiring, plumbing, and the heating, but the problems continued to mount.

It was during this final stage in the life of the Royal Hotel that Ken Fousek made his home in a fourth-floor apartment for eight years, from July 1984 until July 1992. While living at the hotel, Fousek experienced increasing activity that he describes as paranormal phenomena from the hallway outside his apartment. He frequently heard his name called by a male voice emanating from the hall, always in the middle of the night.

> A voice would call my name, "Ken," just outside my apartment door, around two or three in the morning. It wasn't a loud or frightening voice, nor did it seem angry or in any way impatient. But, the mysterious man's voice was loud enough to wake me from my sleep on many, many different occasions.

Fousek requires assistance from a wheelchair, so on those late nights when the disembodied voice would call, there was a considerable amount of time needed for Ken to get from his bed, into his wheelchair, across the apartment, and open his front door. It isn't difficult to understand why at first Ken just assumed that the reason no one was in the hallway when he opened the door was because it had taken him so long to get to the door open. But the strange voice continued to call from the hallway, often up to several times a month, much to the annoyance of Ken. "Perhaps someone is playing a trick," he thought. "Or maybe someone is getting the apartments mixed up, and another Ken lives somewhere in the building."

Finally, after a considerable amount of time had passed, Ken happened to be up late one night. Since he is an avid historian, it is easy to assume Ken was engrossed in a history book, and the time simply got away from him. Ken states:

Royal Hotel, Excelsior Springs, Mo.

This c. 1910 postcard of the exterior of the Royal Hotel features the completed expansion. The additional building to the west and the terra-cotta garden on the roof are clearly visible along with the shops in the front of the building along the street. (From the private collection of Jim Masson.)

THE ROOF GARDEN, ROYAL HOTEL.
EXCELSIOR SPRINGS, MO.

In line with the modern therapy treatments offered at the hotel, this top-floor garden area, pictured around 1910, was perfect for sunbathing and relaxation. The rooftop also offered guests a panoramic view of Excelsior Springs. (From the private collection of Betty Bissell.)

The voice called my name again, "Ken," just like always, from right outside the door. The difference was that this time I was right there by the door and able to open it within seconds. And, of course, once again there was no one in sight. My apartment was right in the middle of the hallway, and I could see clearly down the hallway corridors in each direction. There wasn't time for someone to run away and hide. Even if they had tried, I would have heard their footsteps running down the wooden floor in the hall. From then on, I knew it was a ghost calling to me in the middle of the night. The oddest part was that the ghost actually called to me by my name!

Ken was one of the last residents to live at the Royal Hotel. The building now stands abandoned as a tribute to another and perhaps grander time. Unfortunately for ghost hunters, this large sprawling complex is currently off-limits to the public, making it impossible to host a paranormal investigation. One can, however, drive slowly past the block-long Royal Hotel, but be careful to watch out for the one-way street in front. Or, if a closer and more thorough look at this building is absolutely required, park at the Hall of Waters and walk directly one block west. Have a camera and tape recorder handy; take plenty of pictures of the outside of the building and have the voice recorder at the ready. You might just find upon review a ghost peering from a window or your name called out on your tape recorder.

A special thanks goes out to Ken Fousek, a longtime resident of Excelsior Springs and well-respected member of the community, for stepping forward and allowing his name and his personal ghost story to appear in this book.

From the 1980s until the final closing of the Royal Hotel in the late 1990s, the property was divided into 40 apartments and 45 hotel rooms. The building is currently badly in need of repair. No public access is allowed, but the exterior can be viewed along South Street. (Author's collection.)

This early-1900s postcard is of the downtown district along Broadway Street looking west. It features horse-drawn carriages along the packed-earth roadway. (From the private collection of Betty Bissell.)

Three

THE HALL OF WATERS DISTRICT

THE ATLAS BAR AND THE EXCELSIOR CLUB

The Atlas Bar was established in 1894. Breaking local tradition, the businesses started in this building did not focus on the healing properties of the mineral waters flowing from the multiple springs in town. Instead, there were two ventures giving their attention to the more immediate needs of the gentlemen visitors in the area. On the main floor, this location is rumored to be one of the very first bars in the Midwest constructed by the Joseph Schlitz Brewing Company to carry its line of products. Upstairs on the second story was the Excelsior Club. This second business was accessible only by a separate entrance and private stairway, for it was the home of the local brothel.

Undocumented rumors testify that Joseph Wingate Folk, who served as the 31st governor of Missouri from 1905 to 1909, made it a personal mission to shut down the Excelsior Club. He was known as Gov. "Holy Joe" Folk, due in part to his strict Baptist upbringing and to his reputation as a reformer for attacking corruption and the local party machines when he served earlier in his career as a prosecutor in St. Louis, Missouri. Reports state Governor Folk was only successful in shutting down the operations of the Excelsior Club for a short period of time and that the closure may have come at a time when the Excelsior Club was operating out of the nearby Arlington Hotel.

According to owner Cara, the Atlas Bar was open for business during the 1920s under the name of Al's Diner. She also strongly suspects that the alcoholic beverages portion of the business survived and in all probability thrived during the years of American Prohibition from 1920 to 1933.

Cara is one of the present-day owners of the latest incarnation of the Atlas Bar. She invited me and fellow ghost hunter Joe Kline to visit on a summer Sunday afternoon. Due to Missouri liquor laws, many bars throughout the state are closed on Sundays. For an owner like Cara, this means that Sunday is a great day to clean and prepare for the upcoming week. It is also a convenient opportunity to catch up on paperwork. On this day, she greeted us with a friendly, warming smile and offered us both a fresh-brewed cup of coffee.

Excelsior Springs: Haunted Haven

The current interior of the Atlas was an amazing site to see, for Cara and her co-owners have worked over the course of the past eight years to carefully restore the building to much of its former glory. The first of these finds was the intact tin ceiling tiles that had been hidden away and thankfully preserved for years beneath a drop ceiling. The original mosaic floor tiles, although showing some wear after over 100 years of use, have been carefully cleaned and reset for customers of today. On either end of the bar, two-and-a-half-foot-tall golden art deco female figurine lamps stand majestically, each bearing the Schlitz globe shining above their heads. Other memorabilia from days gone by have been sought out and restored, enhancing the visitors' experience of the past. The nearly 40-foot-long wooden bar, along with the bartender's display cabinets, had been left to suffer the abuses of a century of bar patrons. After much patience and painstaking repair, this massive bar now gleams as the centerpiece of the Atlas Bar and waits for thirsty guests to pull up a stool.

Cara began the visit with a tour. She carefully pointed out the wide variety of historic black-and-white photographs from Excelsior Springs' past displayed on many of the walls, including a photograph of the original Excelsior Club. She also led her guests to the bricked-over doorway that was once the entrance to the private business above. Cara explained that the stairs to the previous upstairs business venture have long since disappeared, "They were probably taken out sometime after a fire ravished the second story." She went on to further explain that the fire took place while the brothel was still in full operation. "Many workers at the Atlas Bar feel that our ghost is a former employee who lost her life in the flames while plying her trade and still haunts the customers at the bar today." The second story was never replaced, but the ghost of the Atlas Bar may be still around tending to her business. They have started calling the additional member of their staff "Ginger." According to Cara, the name just seems to fit.

Cara is not frightened by possibility that the Atlas Bar, where she has devoted so much of her time, may be haunted. In reference to the ghost, Cara states that she seems "very peaceful and a natural fit for these surroundings." It may be that since Cara lives in nearby Ray County, in a historic farmhouse that is also haunted, she is more accustomed to things that go bump in the night. We will not report the address of her home in this publication out of respect for our gracious host, but it was formerly owned by an uncle of Bob Ford, the infamous killer of Jesse James. It is rumored that Bob and his brother Charles spent some time living in the house as well, but this has yet to be verified.

Ghosts have not always been a topic of discussion at the Atlas Bar. Most of the reported paranormal activity seemed to begin during the most recent phase of renovations, when the Atlas was converted from its most recent stint as the Downtowner Bar. One of the first otherworldly experiences happened when Cara was working on a Sunday afternoon, locked in the building alone for peace and quiet doing paperwork. It was in November 2009 when Cara began hearing footsteps and doors opening and closing. These noises did not catch her attention at first, because she had thought the sounds were coming from the neighboring businesses until she realized that it was a Sunday afternoon and none of the nearby shops were open.

On another Sunday afternoon, she heard someone in the restroom. The sound was so clear that Cara was certain her husband had secretly let himself in the building and was trying to play a trick on her. But when she opened the door, she found no one was there.

Cara is not the only one at the Atlas Bar who has reported an encounter with the feminine phantom. Employees frequently report small objects moved from their last station only to turn up later in the most unexpected of places. Several employees have reported repeated experiences with swinging kitchen doors. The rule at the Atlas is to keep the doors closed, but often the doors reopen by themselves when no one is near.

Jae is the beautiful dark-haired manager of the Atlas, and very early one morning she was walking from the kitchen to the bar caring two large buckets heavy with ice. She had filled

The sign for the Atlas can be seen on the right of this early-1900s parade photograph. Excelsior Springs hosted frequent parades to delight the visitors in the area. This tradition of downtown public events along Broadway Street continues today. (From the Atlas Bar Collection.)

Although this 1940s photograph of a fire down the block appears to be a double exposure, the Atlas Bar, complete with the Schlitz globe on top of the building, can be seen in the left corner. (From the Atlas Bar Collection.)

This photograph, taken in the 1950s, provides a good front and side view of the two-story building. The Schlitz globe could still be seen adorning the top of the structure. (From the Atlas Bar Collection.)

Those who have seen of the ghost of Ginger at the Atlas report that she looks similar to the woman in this early advertisement. This gilded framed picture hangs appropriately in the center of the bricked-over doorway that once served as the entrance to the brothel upstairs. (Photograph by Joe Kline.)

the buckets in the kitchen, and although she was alone in the saloon at the time, purely out of habit she shut the swinging kitchen doors behind her when she entered. When Jae approached the swinging doors she was taken by surprise. They slowly opened up as if by some unseen hand to let her pass. As soon as she entered the bar area, the doors slowly and silently closed behind her.

On one occasion Jae actually caught a glimpse of what she feels was Ginger in a reflection in the mirror behind the bar. She was facing the mirror and saw a shadowy, bluish figure standing near in the area of the back entrance next to the arcade machine. She describes the experience as literally taking her breath away—not frightening, but unforgettable. Jae said the woman wore long hair that fell loosely about her shoulders. She was also well endowed and wore a long-sleeved gown that was a pale bluish color and shear. When she turned around to see if anyone was standing in the doorway, the woman had vanished. Jae pointed to a picture hanging on the wall of a scantily dressed woman and explained that the ghostly apparition looked a lot like the woman in the picture.

Both Jae and Cara have been informed by various bar patrons that this picture tends to go in and out of clarity, mostly depending on the number of patrons in the bar. When at its busiest, filled to capacity with customers, guests sitting at the bar have reported noticing the picture becomes eerily sharp and clear. It is during these times that some have been known to sit at the bar and watch for Ginger's invisible ghostly attempts to catch the attention of the men in the room. Jae stated, "You can almost see the shivers go down their spines. Men will twist and turn to see who it was that just tapped them on their shoulders or blew into their ear, only to find no one there."

A female bar patron reported some uncomfortable gestures that she blamed on the unwelcome attention of the ghost in the bar. Cara explained that this event occurred early in March, and the woman was sitting on a stool up against the bar. The patron was seated second from the south end with an empty chair on her left and her boyfriend directly to her right.

Cara gave her guests a visual demonstration of the incident as it was reported to her by the female customer. Tilting the bar stool at nearly a 45-degree angle, she explained that the empty bar stool leaned itself way over and bumped the woman several times on her leg. After the first rude bump, she jumped up and let her boyfriend and the bartender know what had occurred. The two men then both noticed the stool move itself sideways and roughly bump into her chair a second time. Perhaps the ghost wanted the woman's boyfriend all to herself.

Even after this occurrence, the couple decided to stay at the bar and continue to enjoy their drinks, laughing about the episode. And it didn't stop them from keeping the Atlas as their favorite watering hole. As frequent visitors, they really did not think anything further would happen. Six months later, when seated at the bar, the woman was confronted with the ghostly presence once again. This time, she clearly experienced someone coldly blowing down the nape of her neck, sending chills down her spine.

The female spirit known as Ginger has repeatedly stopped the jukebox from playing a particular song. She doesn't like "Nights in White Satin" by the Moody Blues. Every time the song has been selected by a bar patron, the CD inside the old jukebox jumped out of the player and landed somewhere deep inside the machine. When a brand-new jukebox was brought into the Atlas Bar, Cara was hopeful that the days of the Moody Blues disc flying about inside the machine were over. But even with the new machine, the disc continued to jump up and out of the player. The jukebox has only very recently been replaced with a digital Internet music box.

Cara was hoping to see if anyone would come to the bar and be brave enough to download the song to see if it would play. For some unknown reason, "Nights in White Satin" by the Moody Blues seems to be strangely unavailable through the new Internet music system. Many have searched for it, but no one has found it yet. The song itself may provide a few small clues as to why this former "working woman" might not be comfortable with the tune. "Nights in White

Excelsior Springs: Haunted Haven

Satin" was written by a member of the Moody Blues after he was given satin bed sheets by a friend as a gift. Phrases included in the lyrics could easily be interpreted as describing someone longing for love and of someone regretting missed opportunities in life.

Cara told us of a personal experience that took place in June 2010. As before, it was a Sunday afternoon, and she was locked away inside the Atlas working on her paperwork as usual. She had settled herself in near the center of the bar with a small mound of paperwork spread out in front of her. She set her purse on the countertop of the bar to the right of her. To keep herself going, Cara was drinking her usual fresh cup of strong coffee.

Her coffee was low on sugar, and when Cara looked at the sugar canister, she found it was empty. She made a short trip to the kitchen to refill the sugar and her cup. She came back to her workstation, leaving the sugar canister behind on the kitchen counter, and went immediately back to her duties.

Much later in the day, when it was time for her to leave, Cara cleaned up her paperwork and was headed for the door. Picking up her purse, she made an astonishing discovery. There, beneath her purse that had sat at her side on top of the bar for the past three or more hours, was a layer of sugar nearly a quarter of an inch thick.

Cara remembered that the sugar canister had been empty when she reached to use it earlier. And now both the sugar and the canister were still sitting in the kitchen. So when and how this layer of sugar came to be beneath her purse is still a mystery. Cara feels it may be the ghost of the woman upstairs. In her own words, "It honestly felt to me as though the ghost wanted me to know she was happy with the renovations on her home."

Perhaps the most remarkable story of haunting activity at the Atlas Bar occurred near the end of the most recent round of renovations. The Atlas was closed completely during the winter of 2009–2010. Nearing the time to reopen, last-minute details were in frenzy.

Among the most important details is a sizable list of required legal documents to post in clear view for inspectors to review. For safety and ease of reading and for meeting their legal requirements, Cara had purchased a large poster frame and gathered the notices together to display in one easy-to-find location.

"The problem was with the poster itself. Once we hung it on the wall, every week we would find it taken down and set on the floor," Cara explained. The frame was thick metal, and it was about two feet wide and three and a half feet tall with a glass front. "If it had fallen, it would easily break and shatter into pieces. But, every week, we found it taken off the wall and set aside. We had to keep hanging it back up. It was really starting to get annoying. Then one day while we were putting it back on the wall, I noticed the blank space. I had accidently left out the most important document of all, our liquor license. It was a quick fix but if the ghost hadn't pointed out my error, we could have been closed down for not having it in clearly displayed."

Historic buildings have often experienced ghostly activity during renovations, but at the Atlas it would appear the paranormal activity increased after the completion of repairs that resulted in the reopening of the kitchen. Myrna is far more than a waitress at the Atlas, for she is also the cook, sometimes the bartender, and generally the welcoming committee for any stranger who walks through the door. She took time away from her busy schedule to talk about her recent haunting experiences while working in the kitchen.

One of the first tricks Ginger played on Myrna was to steal knives that were left on the kitchen counter one by one. Myrna keeps knives on the end of counter so they are handy while she is busy cooking for customers. At the end of this particular workday, a total of five knives had silently disappeared and were nowhere to be found. Myrna was aware of Ginger's reputation for mischief and was not frightened. Eventually, after much searching, all five knives turned up cleaned and washed and put safely away in their place in the kitchen drawer.

Just a few days later, the daily lunch special was fried pork tenderloins. This special turned out to be very popular, and five orders came into the kitchen at once. Myrna dropped five tenderloins into the hot fryer, but only minutes later two turned up missing. She fished around in the clear, hot frying grease, but the tenderloins had completely vanished right from under her nose.

Myrna now enters the kitchen each day announcing, "Honey, I'm home," in an attempt to slow down the helping hand of her invisible assistant. One day, Ginger let her know that she oversees even the smallest of changes to the routine in the kitchen. Myrna had just finished washing all the lids for the pots and pans and put them away in their usual spot, which is a large plastic tub similar to the type that restaurants use when busing tables. She had trouble fitting in the largest lid, so without thinking Myrna stored it someplace else in the kitchen. She then went back out into the bar to wait on patrons of the Atlas.

Some time had passed before Myrna was able to slip back into the kitchen. When she returned, she found all of the freshly cleaned lids spread out on the floor. Myrna had to take the time to wash, dry, and carefully pack them away. This time, taking note of Ginger's correction, she returned all of the lids to the tub, including the large one. That seemed to solve the problem. Ginger must have been satisfied with the results, for the lids have not been bothered since.

Cara is grateful for the assistance of her unseen employee and hopes guests to the Atlas Bar will have the opportunity to meet the ghost as well. Recently, Cara allowed ghost tours hosted by Paranormal Adventures USA to begin each of their events at this historic haunted location.

Atlas Bar & Grill
100 West Broadway Street
Excelsior Springs, MO 64024
Phone: (816) 630-9229

BROADWAY COMPLEX

The lot at 244 East Broadway Street started its history as property of the City of Excelsior Springs. In 1905, there was a small building on one corner of the property that housed the fire department along with two hand hose carts and one hand hook-and-ladder truck. In 1908, the city started planning to construct a library and restroom on the property. The city being short of funds to complete the project, the Ladies Civic Improvement Association stepped in and held fundraisers to assist in the construction, which was completed in June 1909.

Over the course of the first 40 years, 244 East Broadway Street was home to the Fraternal Order of the Eagles lodge hall on the second floor, the Commercial Club and the Excelsior Springs Military Band in 1917, the American Legion in 1922, and the Clay County Relief Committee in 1940.

This building was well known to visitors to Excelsior Springs up until the 1940s as the location of the public restrooms. Guests to the area met with local physicians and were provided with a list of various mineral spring waters to drink in accordance to treating their particular ailments. The springs were to be visited by the patients in a specific order at varying locations throughout the city and varying times throughout the day. Patients walking from well to well and drinking large amounts of water naturally found themselves at one point or another at the "Public Comfort Station."

The building at 246 East Broadway Street is located in Kugler Lane at the intersection of Broadway, the city having closed the street. Dr. Hiram Clark had the building constructed for his

In 1908, planning began for a public library and restroom facility at 244 East Broadway Street. The Ladies Civic Improvement Association held fundraisers to assist and construction of the new public library, pictured here in the 1910s, was completed in 1909. (From the private collection of Richard Preator.)

Although exaggerated, this historic postcard clearly shows the necessity of a public restroom in Excelsior Springs. Patients were often given prescriptions to travel from spring to spring partaking of the various types of mineral waters, thus creating the dire need for public facilities. (From the private collection of Betty Bissell.)

office and residence in 1909. Dr. Clark attended to the health needs of the citizens of Excelsior Springs until his death on October 2, 1940. He was found by Faye Steele sitting in his chair at his office at 246 East Broadway Street having died from a heart attack.

The second-floor apartment contains many historic architectural details: an impressive white glazed brick fireplace with an ornate brass summer cover over the firebox; decorative wrought iron that supports the oak mantel; sliding pocket doors separating the living areas; and the bedroom and dining room that are illuminated by skylights.

During restoration of the building in 2008, a small tin soda can was found hidden in the basement on a ledge behind a post. Inside the can were two unusual items: a jeweled pour spout like one would use to pour liquor and a small bottle about a quarter full of a dark liquid. On the west side of the basement is a crawl space about two feet wide that was not excavated due to the city water lines that ran down Kugler Lane. Owner Richard Preator states:

> In regards to spirits in 246, for the most part, they have been playful. Recently I rescued some stuffed animals from a trash dumpster and had laid them on front window seat. The next morning as I went about my work I entered the room, and as I walked towards the rear, I heard this funny quacking noise. As I turned to look towards the animals, the noise stopped; as I approached the window seat I spied this little yellow duck, which I suspected to be the culprit. I could tell by squeezing that there was a noisemaker inside, but I could not get it to work. Later that evening, the same noise came from the duck without my being close to it, so out of curiosity, I picked it up and took it upstairs and laid it on my night table. Well wouldn't you know about 5:30 a.m. this duck quacked again about four times, just enough to get me awake. I laughed, rolled over, and went back to sleep. I ended up removing the noisemaker and threw it away after new batteries and tinkering with it failed to produce any noise.

The building at 248 East Broadway Street has had a multitude of incarnations, including housing a bank and later a grocery store. The most recent use of this building was as a beauty school. A fire completely destroyed the building housing Shelton's Flooring next door to the east in March 2008 and caused extensive water and smoke damage to the beauty school.

Richard Preator purchased 246 and 248 East Broadway Street after the fire. During the first stages of cleaning up the smoke and water damage, several encounters with the ghostly residents of the buildings occurred.

At first, Richard tried to convince himself that the building he owned wasn't haunted. There were small occurrences that he decided to overlook or chalk up to clumsiness. He said:

> I was busy working on the window seat in this front office area. I was pulling out a nail, and though applying little force, the nail shot out and hit me in the forehead with such force that it stunned me and blood ran down into my eye. It just wasn't physically right.

One of the most interesting encounters happened while Richard was away on business, and his brother-in-law Ted Cone was overseeing the renovations. In one of the back rooms of 248, a local teenager, Sean, was working alone. Ted was out on the sidewalk when Sean burst out the front door at a full run, clearly shaken and scared. He related to Ted that while in the back room removing old carpet he had felt a hand on his shoulder. Thinking it was a coworker, he turned his head, but there was no one in the room except for himself. He wasted no time extricating himself from the premises.

This c. 1920 photograph showcasing yet another grand parade down Broadway Street was taken in front of Dr. Clark's medical office. His sign can be seen hanging outside the entrance to 246 East Broadway. (From the private collection of Richard Preator.)

Constructed in 1906, the Clay County State Bank was designed by the famous architect Louis S. Curtiss. This building, pictured around 1910, currently houses the Excelsior Springs Museum and Archives. It features architectural detailing that has been painstakingly restored and preserved by countless volunteers in the community. (From the Excelsior Springs Museum and Archives Collection.)

A few days later, Richard was walking through the front waiting room of 248 when a momentary loud blast of music startled him. Spinning to see where the noise came from, he observed a boom box radio quietly sitting in the corner. Of course it was turned off, and by this time he had learned to accept the strange happenings; he spoke out loud, "Yes, I hear you!"

From that point on, Richard learned to respond to the strange happenings and found it easier to speak to the possible spirits, always assuring them that he was only there to preserve and protect the buildings.

EXCELSIOR SPRINGS MUSEUM AND ARCHIVES

No trip to Excelsior Springs would be complete without a visit to the Excelsior Springs Museum and Archives. Visitors to the museum can discover the amazing history of the area, which has been painstaking preserved by those who love and care for their community. These devoted docents, researchers, and volunteers bring the past to life once more while carefully preserving the integrity of their city's story.

Showcasing Excelsior Springs' past and present as a tourist resort, the museum features an extensive historical postcard collection. These postcards feature scenes from the many springs and hotels that once solely drove the local economy. Researchers will be happy to discover complete local newspaper archives dating back to 1903. Genealogists are welcome to utilize the extensive collection of birth, death, marriage, and burial records stored at this location. Veterans and patriots alike should take the time to pause and reflect in the Veteran's Room. Artifacts in this area of the museum commemorate residents of Excelsior Springs who have served and, in many cases, given their lives in defense of their country.

The collections and displays at the Excelsior Springs Museum and Archives are impressive, including the painstaking restoration and preservation of the two-building complex that houses them. It is even more astounding when one takes into consideration that the entire museum, including the welcoming face when one walks in the door, is based completely on volunteer efforts. The monies for utilities, updates, displays, and repairs come entirely from income received from membership dues, gift-shop sales, and visitors' generous donations.

The home of the Excelsior Springs Museum and Archives consists of two historic buildings, each with its own fascinating history. Constructed in 1906 for a sum of $25,000, 101 East Broadway Street is the former home of the Clay County State Bank. The numerous features of architectural detailing on this building, both on the exterior and the interior, are worthy of making this a must-see location on any visit to Excelsior Springs.

Driving down the main strip of Excelsior Springs on East Broadway Street, the Italian Renaissance style of this structure sets it apart from other buildings in the surrounding area, and the classical temple front easily catches the eye.

Guests taking just a few steps inside the entrance of this former bank building gaze in awe at the extensive detailing on the cylindrical vault ceiling, twinkling gently with 112 electric lights. It has taken years, hundreds of volunteer hours, and a large fundraising effort to restore the ceiling to its former glory. Also included in the restoration efforts was the refurbishing and reinstallation of the original ornate lobby chandeliers. The chandeliers are a perfect highlight of the grandeur of the entrance to the bank.

While looking up, the sizable canvas reproductions of two famous paintings by Jean-François Millet, *The Angelus* and *The Gleaners*, are impossible to miss. Both *The Angelus* and *The Gleaners* were painted by Millet in 1857. The original *Angelus* is housed in the Louvre in Paris. This painting depicts two peasants in the fields near sunset bowing their head in prayer. The original *Gleaners* is housed in the Musée d'Orsay, also in Paris. This painting depicts three peasant women gleaning stray grains by hand after the wheat harvest.

The artist who painted these impressive reproductions, Count Edmond deSzaak, is reported to have arrived in Excelsior Springs around 1919. Historians state that Count deSzaak decided to stay in the United States and obtained commissions to paint murals around the Midwest. He also owned a gallery in Oklahoma City, Oklahoma. Born in Budapest, Hungary, the count studied art in the greatest educational and cultural centers of Europe, including Vienna, Paris, and Rome. Sadly, the murals were never sealed or varnished and have faded slightly over time.

Another dominant feature in the bank lobby is the massive 20,000-pound vault door. In spite of its significant size, the vault door has been balanced to such perfection that it can still be moved at the touch of a single finger. With such impressive details above, it might be easy to overlook the timeworn foot-wells on the floor. There in front of each cashier's booth, indented into the floor, are the impressions of the footsteps of countless customers standing in line over the years.

The architect of this incredible structure was Louis Curtiss, a prolific designer credited with working on over 200 buildings throughout the Midwest. The personal life and individual character of Curtiss often drew as much, if not more, attention than his imaginative designs.

Louis Singleton Curtis was born on July 1, 1865, in Belleville, Ontario. He was the fourth of six children. His father, Don Carlos Curtis, supported the family as a dry goods merchant. In 1883, Louis's father passed away; his mother also passed away just a little over a year later.

Louis Curtis(s) arrived on the scene in Kansas City, Missouri, in 1887 at the age of 22. He came following the expansion of the building industry that was quickly converting the city into a major metropolitan area. Not long after his arrival, he arbitrarily began to add an extra "s" to the end of his name to make himself more memorable.

By 1890, Louis Curtiss started the firm of Gunn and Curtiss with his partner, Fredrick Gunn. The team quickly advanced their firm by gaining commissions on many large public projects. These projects stretched across the country, with notable accomplishments in Chicago, Illinois; Forth Worth, Texas; and Huntington, West Virginia.

While becoming very successful in his business life, Curtiss's personal life proved him to be a very colorful individual. He always wore white suits, smoked monogrammed Turkish cigars, and paid his bills in gold coins. Along with many other notables of the day, he also took up an interest in spiritualism.

Just a year prior to beginning work on the Clay County State Bank, Louis was viewing a fire in the West Bottoms area of Kansas City and reportedly was exposed to smallpox. This incident required confinement for several months. It was after this dramatic event in his life that his architectural work took on a far more personalized style. This change is clearly evident in the exacting detail work in the barrel-vaulted ceiling within the bank.

In 1906, Louis Curtiss completed work on the Clay County State Bank and the El Bisonte Hotel in Hutchison, Kansas. Sadly, in December of this same year, he also proposed marriage to a longtime family friend, Grace Griffin, only to be rejected. Grace very quickly married a man from England. In spite of this setback in his personal life, Louis continued to thrive as an architect. In 1919, he was called upon to work on the bank building once more to design an expansion. The expansion added four feet to the west, eight feet to the east, and several additional feet to the south. The reopening of the grand bank building took place in 1920.

Just one year prior to the expansion work on the original bank building, an incredible act of patriotism took place on Main Street running directly along the west side of the building. A public auction was held on the roadway beginning at Broadway Street and stretching several

The exacting detail work of architect Louis S. Curtiss can be seen on the former Clay County State Bank's cylindrical ceiling, featuring 112 electric lights. It has taken hundreds of volunteer hours to restore this ornate ceiling. Included in the restoration project were the ornate lobby chandeliers. (Author's collection.)

This photograph of Louis S. Curtiss was taken near the time of his arrival in Kansas City, Missouri, in 1887 at the age of 22 to begin his historical architectural career. (From the Kansas Collection, Spencer Research Library, University of Kansas.)

This photograph was taken on March 16, 1918, at an auction for the Red Cross war effort in France. The picture was taken on South Main Street facing west toward Spring Street. The items auctioned were from the James family farm in nearby Kearney, Missouri, and were donated by Frank James's son Robert James three years after his father's death. (From the Missouri Valley Special Collections, Kansas City Public Library, Kansas City, Missouri.)

blocks south, ending at the intersection of South Street. The date was Saturday, March 16, 1918, and the auction was being held as a benefit for the Red Cross of Excelsior Springs to aid the war effort in France.

Although the cause was noble, it was the items for sale that brought crowds out onto the streets that day. For sale were many items from the James family farm and a few personal items belonging to Frank and Jesse James. According to a follow-up article printed in the *Excelsior Springs Daily Standard*, the items sold at auction were donated by Robert James, the son of the Frank James. Robert James had refused to sell any of the family heirlooms at any price since the passing of his father just three years earlier.

Among the items sold was a musket with the name "Frank James" carved deep into the stock. The newspaper article reads:

> Most of the older residents of Clay County who attended the auction were surprised to find that Robert James, son of Frank James, and who now conducts the James farm, had consented to part with the weapon which his father had carried through all the days of guerilla warfare, and his later bandit career.

The article later quotes Robert James as stating, "My father would rather have seen the gun put to the services of the Red Cross than be put to any other use."

Also sold were two six-shooters reportedly used by Frank and Jesse along with an older bullet mold from the farm. Even a few personal items of Zerelda Samuels, the mother of Frank and Jesse James, were bid upon, including a candlestick mold, two spinning wheels, and a flax reel. Astoundingly, a gold shirt stud worn by Jesse James at the time of his death was auctioned off for the high price of $31.

The monies raised from the auction sales were slated by the Red Cross for the purchase of hundreds of yards of muslin to be shipped overseas for use as bandages for wounded soldiers. As a constant reminder of the cause for which all were assembled, women wearing the Red Cross white veils of service stood around the auctioneer's platform. Additionally, many local residents contributed to the fundraising efforts by donating their own canned goods, farm produce, and livestock to the auction. Those fortunate enough to visit the Excelsior Springs Museum and Archives are encouraged to take the short stroll along the side of the museum, down the sidewalk on Main Street, and picture for themselves the patriotic pride and public sacrifices made by Robert James and so many other Excelsior Springs residents that day so long ago.

Controlling interest in the Clay County State Bank was purchased by William T. Kemper Sr. and Sons in 1932. The William Kemper family is credited with developing United Missouri Bank (UMB) and Commerce Bancshares, along with many other successful investments throughout the Midwest. The purchase of the Clay County State Bank occurred less than three years after the great crash of the New York Stock Exchange. Forever known as "Black Friday," October 29, 1929, was the beginning of the Great Depression. R. Crosby Kemper, the eldest son of William Kemper Sr., was president of City National Bank and Trust Company during this time. He personally described the difficulties the banking industry faced as a growth experience:

> I could not imagine more interesting times than this period from 1929 to 1933. Men who have survived have learned more than they learned in any other ten years of their business lives. I know I have. Without going through that period no man could have any conception of how fast things could slump or of how fast they could come back.

In 1950, the front facade of the bank was altered slightly to make the building accessible to the handicapped. Very little of the outward appearance was changed to make these much-needed accommodations. In 1968, the Clay County State Bank constructed a new bank building, the Excelsior Springs Savings & Loan. The former bank location was donated to the City of Excelsior Springs for use as a museum.

If one key figure stands out in the history of the Clay County State Bank and the Excelsior Springs Museum and Archives, it is Sam C. Sherwood. In an article published in the *Kansas City Star* in 1978, Sam C. Sherwood was identified as the "unofficial town historian" of Excelsior Springs. In 1987, the *Excelsior Springs Daily Standard* stated that Sam was a "walking, talking encyclopedia of Excelsior Springs' history." These statements were more than just flattering words. Sam Sherwood rightfully earned his distinctive place in Excelsior Springs' history for having worked so diligently throughout his life to research, document, and promote his beloved town's story.

In 1904, at the age of 10, Sam Sherwood arrived with his family in Excelsior Springs from his original hometown of Abilene, Kansas. In 1916, Sam was employed as a bookkeeper with the Clay County State Bank. He left the bank for a period beginning in 1917 to serve in the air service of the US Army. It was while Sam was away fulfilling his patriotic duty that the James family auction took place alongside of the bank to raise funds for the Red Cross to aid soldiers wounded in the line of duty.

When Sam returned to Excelsior Springs, he also returned to his civilian duties at the Clay County State Bank and soon became an assistant cashier. He remained an employee of the bank during the transition when the bank became a part of the larger Commerce Bank family. Sam Sherwood later became a charter member on the Excelsior Springs Museum Board. He also served as president of the organization for five years.

Sam served the community in a multitude of capacities, so many that the following listing is only a portion of his vast accomplishments. During his life, he served as president for the Excelsior Springs centennial celebration, served on the Excelsior Spring Historic Preservation Commission, was a trustee of the Barbee Memorial Presbyterian Church, served as second commander of the Clyde Gustine post of the America Legion, was a member of the chamber of commerce, was a member of the Boy Scout area board, was a member of Kiwanis, and also was essential to the formation the Excelsior Springs Savings and Loan Association.

Sam continued over the years as a devoted researcher and volunteer extraordinaire, dedicating countless hours to the Excelsior Springs Museum and Archives. He assisted in the acquisition of editions of the *Excelsior Springs Daily Standard* dating back to the early 1900s, which was essential when researching this publication.

Visitors to the museum may be awed by the foot wells at the base of the cashiers' windows, impressions left from years of customers standing in line to tend to their daily banking business, and never realize that the actions and perseverance of Sam Sherwood have made a lasting impression on the history of Excelsior Springs.

Another key figure in the early years of the Clay County State Bank was Dr. William Stone Woods. Dr. Woods had been a fixture in the bank for several years, with his own office where he oversaw the financial interests of multiple banking projects in the Kansas City region. He also set up permanent residence at the historic Elms hotel. Records indicate that in 1917, the same year that Sam Sherwood enlisted in the armed forces, Dr. Woods was an officer of the bank.

Dr. Woods led a remarkable life. His financial prowess over the course of his life brought his business ventures to the forefront of the US banking industry. He also left behind a legacy and a dynasty that continues to thrive today.

Much of Dr. Woods's experiences have been chronicled, partly due to his being a major benefactor and namesake of William Woods University in Blue Springs, Missouri. Details from an article dated the fall/winter of 1999 from the *William Woods University Alumni Magazine*,

Sam Sherwood dedicated much of his life to researching and promoting Excelsior Springs's history. He was first employed at the bank in 1916, and with the exception of time spent in the armed forces during World War I, he worked in the building his entire career. (From the Excelsior Springs Museum and Archives Collection.)

written by Gary R. Kremer, professor of history, have helped to shed light on this influential historical figure who finished out his years while working at the Clay County State Bank.

William Stone Woods was born on November 1, 1840, in Columbia, Missouri. He graduated from the University of Missouri in 1861 and studied at two medical colleges before beginning his practice in Monroe County, Missouri. He married Albina Jane McBride on July 10, 1866, and evidently ended his medical practice to pursue a more lucrative profession in general merchandising. After managing a grocery business with his brother in 1868, Dr. Woods established the Rocheport Saving Bank. Moving to Kansas City in 1881, he became president of the Kansas City Savings Association, which he reorganized into the Bank of Commerce along with his nephew Chandler and additional business partners. The organization grew to manage up to 18 banking institutions across multiple states by 1903.

Dr. Woods also donated property for the Female Orphans School in Kansas City. A fire in 1890 destroyed the building, and the facility was moved to Fulton, Missouri. In 1900, Dr. Woods paid off the school's mortgage debt, leading the college trustees to rename the institution William Woods College.

William T. Kemper Sr. was hired by Dr. Woods to serve as the vice president of Commerce Bank in Kansas City in 1906. The Commerce Bank, along with many banks throughout the United States, was forced to close its doors during what has come to be known as the Panic of 1907. The nation was facing an economic recession, and depositors who began to lose their confidence in the banking system started a run on many of the largest banks, creating a domino effect resulting in bank closings across the country. William T. Kemper Sr. was able to reorganize the Kansas City–based bank and successfully open the doors under the name of the Commerce Trust Company.

Dr. Williams Stone Woods passed away on July 5, 1917, at the age of 76. He had been residing at the Elms hotel. At the time of his passing, his estate had an estimated value of $5 million. In August of the same year, his granddaughter Gladys Woods Rubey married James Kemper, son of William Kemper Sr., and the two banking families forever became intertwined.

The two buildings that currently comprise the Excelsior Springs Museum and Archives have been conjoined in purpose and design by removing portions of the interior walls on the main floor to form a large and welcoming space for historic displays. While these two buildings have a joint mission of preserving the past, the histories of the two are entirely separate and vastly different from one another.

The second and much larger structure of the Excelsior Springs Museum and Archives is the historic building at 105 East Broadway Street, which is directly east of the ornate bank building. Details gleaned from the City of Excelsior Springs Historical Preservation Commission state that while the main strip of Broadway was developed quickly, the plot of land at 105 East Broadway Street lay undeveloped until 1917. One reason this small strip remained untouched was that it served in the early 1900s a section of the grounds surrounding the Excelsior Hotel. In 1917, the two-story structure with 35 rooms opened its doors at the St. Joe Hotel, advertising "European rooms on Suite with Private Bath." Nellie Kline was the first proprietor of the hotel.

The St. Joe was sold in July 1934 to two private individuals, Francis Parle and Pauline Cunningham. The hotel was renamed the Hotel Francis and reopened with 45 rooms in September of the same year. As a former clerk at the nearby Royal Hotel for eight years, Mrs. Cunningham possessed a good understanding of the needs of the tourists coming to the area as well as a thorough knowledge of the expanding water therapy industry in Excelsior Springs. The newly dubbed Hotel Francis offered its guests rooms with high ceilings and a space with either a bath or toilet. The hotel catered to guests and permanent residents. The advertised price for a week at the Hotel Francis during the 1940s was $3 to $7 on the European plan.

The picture for this postcard was taken in the early 1950s. On the right is the sign for the Clay County State Bank and the Excelsior Institute next door. A large round sign for the Ball Clinic can be seen in the upper left near the middle of the scene. This image was taken near the corner of Broadway and South Main Streets facing east. (From the private collection of Betty Bissell.)

Research suggests that the main entrance to the Hotel Francis was on the south side of the building, while the first floor to the north served as home to several different business ventures over the years. During the earliest years, the first floor was home to Don Shelton Shoes and the Broadway Clothing Company. In latter years, this street-front section of the building was home to Madden's Dry Goods, the Wicker Furniture Company, and the Surplus Furniture Outlet.

The second story of this building became the home of the Excelsior Institute Osteopathic Hospital & Clinic in 1955. The institute specialized in the nonsurgical treatment of prostate, rectal, and allied disorders. The institute was referred to as the Excelsior Medical Clinic from 1963 until 1973. It later moved directly across the street to the northern side of East Broadway. A large vertical sign that once advertised the institute's final location still looms over the north side street as a quiet reminder of the focus on health and natural healing that at one time strengthened the weary and grew the economy of the city.

For a short period of time, the bank expansion section between the two buildings was home the Excelsior Springs Chamber of Commerce. The building at 105 East Broadway Street sat entirely empty and abandoned for many years until scores of local citizens spent countless hours renovating the first floor to become the current annex of the Excelsior Springs Museum and Archives. Their efforts were assisted with additional labor from the Excelsior Springs Job Corps and the Excelsior Springs High School. The annex portion of the museum was complete in 2006.

The eastern portion of the Excelsior Springs Museum and Archives is truly a shining example of the community spirit that continues to thrive in this northwestern Missouri community. The completed and expanded two-building museum complex is truly worthy of inclusion on every tourist's itinerary of "must see" places when visiting Excelsior Springs.

Excelsior Springs Museum and Archives
101 East Broadway Street
PO Box 144
Excelsior Springs, MO 64024
Phone: (816) 630-0101
Hours of Operation:
Tuesday–Saturday
Winter Hours: 11:00 a.m.–4:00 p.m.
Summer Hours: 10:00 a.m.–4:00 p.m.
www.exsmo.com
Research assistance available by contacting museum personnel.

Hall of Waters

Listed in the National Register of Historic Places, it is only fitting that the majestic Hall of Waters can be found at the very heart of Excelsior Springs. The building sits on the original site of Siloam Spring, which was discovered to have healing properties in 1880. It was the first mineral water spring discovered in the area and virtually the birthplace of the city itself.

The original name of this spring was Excelsior Spring. The waters were found to hold high levels of calcium bicarbonate, magnesium bicarbonate, and iron bicarbonate and lower levels of other minerals such as silica, calcium sulphate, and magnesium chloride among others. During the early years, the spring hosted 30 visitors at a time with the additions of a small pump and small pavilion. Improvements continued over the years with further additions of a concrete platform with benches and a larger pavilion structure.

The Hall of Waters—the "World's Longest Water Bar"—is pictured in a 1940s postcard. The extensive water bar was the main draw for visitors to the Hall of Waters. Guests could sample mineral waters from 10 city-owned springs. Many details in the Hall of Waters were created in the Art Deco style, including two massive lamps hanging over the water bar. (From the private collection of Betty Bissell.)

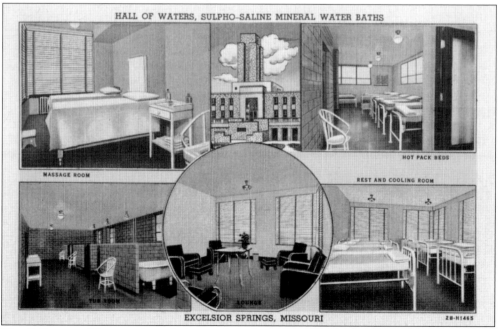

This 1940s postcard depicting the Hall of Waters hydrotherapy showcases some of the services available in the hydrotherapy patients' wing at the Hall of Waters. Some of the medical equipment used from the 1930s until the early 1960s can still be seen by visitors today. (From the private collection of Betty Bissell.)

This postcard depicts the Hall of Waters swimming pool around the 1960s. Due to economic reasons and damage from flooding in 1993, the Olympic-sized swimming pool beneath the World's Longest Water Bar is no longer accessible to the public. This pool was filled mineral water from the White Sulphur Spring. (From the private collection of Brenda Berger.)

A portion of the original hydrotherapy services area of the Hall of Waters remains and can be toured by visitors. This museum area is currently the only location remaining in Excelsior Springs where guests can view a hydrotherapy and massage clinic from the past nearly in its original state. (Author's collection.)

In 1917, two pavilions designed by landscape architect George E. Kessler and architect Henry F. Hoit were erected: the Siloam Spring Pavilion and the Sulpho Saline Pavilion, with the latter's waters pumped from a well to the north. The style chosen for these structures was highly reminiscent of the neoclassical architectural style utilized during the World's Fair of 1904 in St. Louis, Missouri. This is not surprising, since George Kessler was also the landscape architect on the 1904 World's Fair project.

Constructed at a cost of $1 million, the Hall of Waters was a Works Projects Administration (WPA) project. Construction on the building began on May 27, 1936, just one year after the City of Excelsior Springs had purchased the rights to 10 of the area's mineral water springs. The cornerstone was laid in the midst of great ceremony. The ceremonial event was also broadcast by CBS to radio stations across the country. In attendance on that prestigious day were elected officials and local celebrities. Also reported to be in the gathered crowd was the well-known artist Thomas Hart Benton. Benton was a teacher at the nearby Kansas City Art Institute. His artwork had gained attention by this stage in his life, and his self-portrait was featured on the cover of *Time* magazine in December 1934.

When the building was completed in 1937, major features included a water bar, an Olympic-sized swimming pool, separate men's and women's hydrotherapy departments, and a polio therapy pool. The structure is adorned with outstanding examples of the Art Deco style. Just a few examples of the superb workmanship can be seen in the two massive lamps prominently hanging over water bar, the highly stylized elevator doors near the main entrance, and the pairs of sizable lanterns at each exterior entrance. And, with a touch of whimsy and mysticism, reliefs representing eight Mayan warriors were chosen for use on the concrete framing the doorway of main entrance.

Central to the functioning of the Hall of Waters was the extensive water bar. Here visitors and patients alike could sample by the glass the four types of mineral waters pumped in from the 10 individual city-owned springs. Among these was the iron manganese water from the original Siloam Springs well below the building. The various mineral waters were also bottled and shipped to customers around the globe.

To the east of the main lobby, visitors can still stroll through a portion of the hydrotherapy patients' wing. Empty tubs that once provided mineral water baths and bare massage tables, along with a few extraordinary pieces of the medical equipment in use from the 1930s until the early 1960s, help visitors to this museum wing to imagine the Hall of Waters in its glory years. This room stands eerily still as a testament to days gone by when holistic healing and wellness programs went hand in hand with practical medical treatment. Multiple testimonials of healings provided by customers of the mineral baths can be found reprinted in *America's Haven of Health, Excelsior Springs, Missouri's National Health Resort* and *The Waters of Excelsior Springs, Valley of Vitality*. Surprisingly, as of this writing, no paranormal activity has been reported in this section of the building.

Below the main level of the building, underneath the Worlds Longest Water Bar, is where stories of ghostly activity have been reported in this historic location. Here, in what is now an empty shell of an Olympic-sized swimming pool, is where visitors of the past have chosen to remain. This pool was filled mineral water provided by the White Sulphur Spring, located nearby at 505 Elms Boulevard. Some reports state that the oversized balcony area around the pool could seat up to 500 people. The view from the panoramic windows on three sides of the pool featured well-tended gardens.

While the Hall of Waters has been featured in several ghost-story publications, the paranormal activity at the Hall of Waters was witnessed personally by PEDRO team member Joe Kline. The following excerpt is written in his own words:

The Hall of Waters was constructed at a cost of $1 million in 1937 as a WPA project. Features unique to this highly stylized structure are the ornate lanterns at each entrance and reliefs representing eight Mayan warriors used on the framing of the doorway at the main entrance. (Author's collection.)

In all probability, this private residence was the home of Herbert Hope, an undertaker in the early years of Excelsior Springs. The details in the stonework are remarkably similar to the Hope Funeral Home, constructed in the 1930s. (Author's collection.)

I was on a research trip to Excelsior Springs. I was invited to go down and take a look at the currently unused pool. I had seen postcards and pictures of the room before, but little did I know how badly they skewed the scale as I saw just how enormous the place was when I walked out onto the upper balcony.

As I entered the main level of the pool, however, I was surprised even more when, for a brief second, I heard the sound of children playing. As brief as it was, I was still able to make out a child's playful laugh, and the distinct sound of bare wet feet running on concrete. The sound was so clear, that I was taken aback when the room was bare, and the peeling paint and missing tiles showed me a ghost of what once was.

This incident confused me at first, because I had assumed that the pool was for treatment of various ailments, as most of the areas in the rest of the building had been. I was surprised yet again a few days later when I was talking to my grandmother about my trip and she began to reminisce about how her father had taken her swimming there numerous times during her childhood.

The swimming pool at the Hall of Waters has been closed to the public for many years. Much of the current damage was a result of the 1993 flood, which caused extensive destruction in the Midwest.

Seeking additional tales from the historic and haunted Hall of Waters? Chapter 34 of *Haunted Kansas City Missouri* by Angela Cox has other ghostly tales to relate.

City of Excelsior Springs, Missouri
Hall of Waters
201 East Broadway Street
Excelsior Springs, MO 64024
Phone: (816) 630-0752
Hours of Operation:
Monday–Friday
8:00 a.m.–5:00 p.m.
cityofesmo.com

HOPE RESIDENCE AND RELIEF SPRING HOTEL

The small stone one-story home that in all probability was the residence of the Herbert Hope family is located just one block north of the downtown shopping district on Broadway. Herbert Hope was the operator of a leading undertaking business in the early years of Excelsior Springs. Extensive research and comparisons with the 1920 census records narrows down the location of this property within mere feet of the current structure and lends credence to this claim. This private residence can be found near the intersection of West Excelsior Street and North Thompson Avenue.

Herbert Hope and his partner, J.C. Prather, began as the operators of Prather & Hope Undertakers at 203 South Main Street. In the 1930s, the large stone Hope Funeral Home was constructed at nearby 216–220 Spring Street. This stone building is remarkably similar in style and design to the Hope family residence, including the stylized features of stone triangles and obelisks scattered prominently throughout the exterior walls.

Some sources have claimed that these stone triangles and obelisk shapes found so frequently in the masonry of both the private home and the Hope Funeral Home are Masonic in origin. Although nothing has yet been discovered to verify the statement of the home being Masonic in design, Herbert Hope was a member of the Masonic lodge. Being active in the community, he also held memberships with the Modern Woodmen of America, the Benevolent and Protective Order of the Elks, the Christian Church, and the Independent Order of Odd Fellows.

Born in Excelsior Springs on November 2, 1881, Herbert Hope was the son of Thomas Hope, a Civil War veteran from Tennessee. His father operated a local grocery store, owned large amounts of property, and was a city councilman for several years. Herbert's mother, Martha A. (Craven) Hope, was a native of Missouri and passed away in 1906 while Herbert was still a young man. Herbert married Mary La Bena Pence on February 27, 1907. It is not known precisely when the family acquired their beautiful stone estate, but together they raised their children, Mary and Charles.

Herbert worked various jobs during his lifetime, including selling souvenirs, which was a fairly lucrative business in the tourist resort setting of Excelsior Springs. By 1911, Herbert had settled in to a career, which would remain with him for the majority of his life, as the local undertaker. The beautiful Hope Funeral Home still stands along Spring Street silently awaiting its next business venture.

It was a hot and sunny August afternoon in 2010 when Joe Kline and I first met George Moon, RN. Moon is the current owner of the Hope family residence. Joe assisted by bringing along a laptop computer and scanning equipment and basically getting the job of carrying all the heavy equipment. We settled into his comfortable home and were grateful to be allowed to scan a picture.

The image provided by Moon (above, on page 73) and later discovered among the archives of the Excelsior Springs Museum and Archives helped to clearly explain how his home was forever tied to the former location of the Relief Spring Hotel. From 1884 until 1908, during its various stages of construction and growth, the Relief Spring Hotel sat directly behind his property across the Dry Fork of the Fishing River.

Discovered in 1884, Relief Springs was the third mineral water spring to be located in the area after the discoveries of the Regent Spring (formerly Empire Spring) and Siloam Springs. The waters from it contained lithia and calcium. The spring was originally walled in with cobblestones in an effort to safeguard it from the frequent flooding in the area. Visitors could easily fill their cups, jugs, or pails with the mineral water that was claimed to have remarkable properties.

Oddly enough, magnetism was listed among the unusual qualities of the Relief Spring waters. The claim was that any small utensil made of steel left in the basin of the Relief Spring well overnight would emerge with magnetic properties, allowing it to pick up a small metallic object such as a sewing needle or pin.

A small bathhouse was constructed by John Kimber near the spring in 1884. Kimber purchased the spring from Henry C. Fish. In an attempt to garner interest in the springs from the surrounding areas, H.C. Fish began the Relief Springs and Land Company. Eventually this organization became the Excelsior Spring Company. This group worked with funders from nearby Kansas City to aid in the creation of the Elms and the Music Hall and plotted out several residential districts. The company also worked on multiple infrastructure projects within Excelsior Springs. The Excelsior Spring Company soon launched a very successful nationwide marketing campaign to draw visitors to the city. In 1910, Charles Fish and Major Bell worked with landscape architect George Kessler for the General Realty and Mineral Water Company on the Excelsior Springs Golf Course project.

Two years later, in 1886, the property was purchased by Andrew Morgan. By 1888, the property's bathhouse had become a beautiful three-story hotel. For reasons unknown, the business owned

Notations on this photograph describe it as "The Relief Hotel and Springs about 1902." Further descriptive text on the back reads, "Photo by Henry Kasson. Ethil Kasson, the photographer's daughter is in the foreground." A stamp on the back of the picture states, "Excelsior Springs Pictorial, 222 North Kansas City Avenue, Excelsior Springs, Missouri." (From the private collection of George Moon, RN, and the Excelsior Springs Museum and Archives Collection.)

This 1900s photograph depicts the springhouse for the Relief Springs well. It was the third mineral spring located in the area. The spring was originally walled with cobblestones to safeguard it from flooding. Visitors could fill cups with the water, which it was claimed had magnetic properties. (From the Excelsior Springs Museum and Archives Collection.)

by Morgan failed, and the title was scooped up by Kate Vanderwerker. She in turn sold the property to William Fairfield.

A small advertisement in the *Daily Phunn* of Excelsior Springs on Wednesday, July 26, 1893, marketed the Relief Hotel, with J.B. Perkins as the proprietor, stating simply, "Gives Magnetic, Mineral and Mud Baths, $7 per week, $1.50 per day. Including, 'Free Baths to Guests.' "

One newspaper article lists the Relief Spring waters as the Relief Magnetic Spring. This publication states the water was good for such ailments as "female weakness" and obesity. It continues to claim the mineral water helped children with weakness of the urinary organs. An additional article of which the original date has been unfortunately lost to time names the hotel as the Magnetic Sanitarium with proprietors Dr. Etta Semple and Mrs. U.A. McOmber. In this case, the article promotes the hotel as providing "*any treatment* needed for the immediate *care of patients will be given*. We will be ready to receive and care for the most *helpless* cases soon."

In 1901, C.E. Flanders purchased the building and the surrounding two acres of ground for $4,200. He also added $1,000 worth of improvements to his newly acquired property. This investment was reported to net him an income of $900 a year. In 1903, the hotel was being advertised in the *Excelsior Springs Daily Call* as the Marietta Hotel (formerly Relief Springs) with T.C. Patterson as the proprietor. The advertisement promoted the "coolest rooms in the city."

In 1904, Flanders sold the hotel to C.C. Carter for $11,500, including the nearby Flanders's Dry Goods Store in the trade. Information on the spirits still lingering at the former Flanders's Dry Goods Store, which is now Redmond's Home Décor and Furnishings, can be found in a later chapter in this publication. During his ownership of the hotel, Carter invested an additional $3,500 in improvements to the property. He in turn sold the hotel three years later to the Anthropological Sanitarium Company, which was headed by Dr. Orin Robinson. This incarnation is sometimes also referred to by the name of Robinson Sanitarium.

Information gleaned from the handbook provided by the Anthropological Sanitarium to potential patients states that this facility was one of three owned by the organization. Oddly enough, this pamphlet claims that patients can "come to either of these Sanitariums and see thousands of gall stones we have removed without a surgical operation."

The existence of this organization in Excelsior Springs was ended by a devastating fire. The building had been closed by the owners for some 15 months prior for extensive remodeling. According to a report printed in the *Excelsior Springs Daily Call*, it was early in the morning of August 31, 1908, when the Anthropological Sanitarium caught fire and burned to the ground. The paper reported the fire as being the largest the town had seen since the burning of the first Elms hotel in 1898.

Dr. Orin Robertson had arrived in Excelsior Springs the day before at 2:40 p.m. on the Wabash train. Dr. Robertson and a man by the name of Ralph Wade stated that they spent the night in a room on the first floor of the vacant structure. Wade later explained that the pair thought they heard footsteps of someone possibly ransacking the building around 2:00 a.m. They found it difficult to sleep soundly after the possible intrusion, and around 4:30 a.m. they awoke to the sound of cracking flames and the strong smell of smoke.

The two dressed so quickly to escape the flames that Dr. Robertson made it outside in his bare feet, having forgotten to put on his shoes in the ensuing dash for safety. An alarm was quickly raised, but it would be another 15 minutes before the firemen arrived with the hose wagon to fight the flames. Since the nearest fire hydrant was approximately 600 feet away, the water pressure coming from the hose at such a distance was greatly decreased, further slowing down the efforts of the firemen to dowse the flames. The efforts to contain the growing inferno were focused on the south end of the building.

Another hydrant was tapped, also at a great distance, in an attempt to work on the blaze from the northern end of the hotel as well. The span of several hundred feet from the second hydrant

At one point in the late 1890s, Relief Springs Hotel, depicted in this 1890s line drawing, was renamed the Magnetic Sanitarium. The proprietors, Dr. Etta Semple and Mrs. U.A. McOmber, promoted the facility as able to provide care for the most helpless of cases. (From the Excelsior Springs Museum and Archives Collection.)

to the northern walls of the Relief Spring Hotel required someone returning to city hall for an additional length of fire hose. The delay in hooking up the second line cost the firemen another 10 precious minutes.

Only moments after the second fire hose was pressed into service, the framework of the hotel began to collapse. The upper floors started to crash down, barely missing the firemen with their freshly attached hose on the northern side. The *Excelsior Springs Journal* reported later that same day, "When the tin roof fell in, the deafening crash sent a mighty cloud of flaming sparks high into the air and for the moment it seemed inevitable that the conflagration would spread despite all the firemen could do."

The blaze grew to such proportions that by 5:30 a.m. the firemen were forced to back away from the intense flames and turn their focus on preventing the fire from spreading to other structures in the area. Obviously, the entire building was a loss. Papers reported that Dr. Robertson was hopeful of rebuilding in the future.

An article in the October 13, 1911, *Excelsior Springs Daily Call* states that plans were being made to improve the land at the Relief Spring Hotel. The new proprietors were Prof. J.F. Kennedy, Dr. J.T. Rice, and Rev. J.L. Gresham of the Christian Church. There were plans in place to rebuild the spring pagoda and create a park on the surrounding land. It is unknown at the time of this printing if these plans were successful.

A second well was dug adjacent to the Relief and dubbed the Salax Well. An advertisement appearing in the *Excelsior Springs Daily Call* on August 22, 1912, promoted the individual healing properties of the wells with the following: "SALAX, the Great Purifier, for the stomach and bowels. RELIEF water for the nerves and glandular system. Try them."

With the background in place, we return to our story and to the peaceful home of George Moon. Moon makes no claim to being psychic, nor has he personally ever experienced anything that he would call paranormal. But he is a friendly, kind, and open-minded individual. When he first arrived in Excelsior Springs, he was one of the managing partners of the Center for Natural Therapeutics, which was housed in the former Odd Fellows building on Thompson Street for nearly 10 years. This occupation and his friendly demeanor helped him to become quickly known and welcomed in his new community.

Through his many acquaintances, Moon met a woman who will be referred to in this text as Jennifer. Jennifer wishes to remain anonymous, and the pseudonym seemed fitting in reference to the similarly sweet and attractive Ghost Whisperer of television fame.

Jennifer arrived at the former Hope residence and sat down to share her remarkable story. As a close friend and frequent visitor to the historic home of George Moon, she was quickly aware of the additional presence of a ghostly woman keeping watch over the visitors to the house. Over the course of time, Jennifer became more in tune with the ghost, who eventually identified herself as Irene or sometimes Irenie. This otherworldly resident of the home spoke at a quick pace, and it was often difficult for Jennifer to keep up with the flow of information, but she was able to glean a few facts.

Irene let Jennifer know that she was the mother of a young child named Pauline. Pauline was about five years old when she drowned in the shallow waters of the Dry Fork of the Fishing River directly behind the home. Jennifer explained to us with tears in her eyes that "it was a bright summer day and Irene had patted her little girl on the bottom, gave her a freshly baked cookie, and sent her out to enjoy some fresh air. That was the last time Pauline was ever seen alive."

As Jennifer related the facts, she began to paint a picture in our minds of Irene and her daughter Pauline (or possibly Susanne). Irene appeared to be an older woman with long graying hair that showed streaks of red from former years. When Jennifer describe the child, she saw her laid out for her funeral in a small white pinafore with brownish hair that showed golden highlights from playing in the sun. The description was so real that we were drawn further into her tale.

Jennifer herself is careful to check and double-check her facts when such an experience occurs. She related to us that she journeyed to the banks of the Dry Fork just behind the house. Here on the shoreline Jennifer helped the wandering spirit of Irene to cross over in peace. Then Jennifer whispered a small prayer into the air to find some sort of physical confirmation of the unique experience that had just unfolded before her. Within only half an hour, she was given the picture of Ethil Kasson (see page 73). Ethil did not drown in the Dry Fork waters, but she does appear in a photograph from the same period—approximately the 1910s—gazing longingly at her reflection in the stream. Her father was a well-known local photographer. Along with recording many scenic shots of Excelsior Springs during the booming years of the 1910s and 1920s, he also frequently captured his favorite subject, his daughter Ethil, for prosperity as well.

Only a preliminary search of death records has been done at this time, with few results. Death records from the early 1900s in the area did not contain much information, but a young drowning victim during this time period has yet to be discovered. However, several death certificates of interest were discovered. Two children named Pauline passed away in Excelsior Springs during this time period. The first Pauline died in 1919 at two years of age. The certificate lists the cause of death as "diphthina." The second Pauline passed away in 1913 at the tender age of eight months. Her death certificate lists the cause of death as "bronchil pneumonia." It is interesting to note that the undertaker listed on the certificate for the second Pauline is John C. Prather, the partner of Herbert Hope, who at one time owned the residence.

Hopefully the tale of Irene and her daughter Pauline will come to light in the near future. We did walk along the shoreline of the Dry Fork directly behind George Moon's home. Time has deepened the sides of the ravine, but the basic features of the area were an obvious match to the photograph of the former sight of the Relief Spring Hotel and Bath House. This spot currently contains no construction; only a wooded, grassy clearing and the steep banks of the Dry Fork remain.

George Moon reports that after the intervention of his friend Jennifer, the house is now at peace, and no spirits or apparitions have been reported since. He also feels the house is peaceful due to the helpful, kind, and understanding nature of Herbert Hope, whose livelihood as an undertaker depended on assisting the grieving families and seeing to their departed loved ones.

THE MUSIC HALL

The Music Hall was constructed in 1898 by the Excelsior Springs Company. This large, ornate opera house had seating for up to 1,320 patrons and could be easily seen by guests on the porches of the nearby Elms hotel. That same year, the Royal Hotel just a few blocks to the north and east began its first incarnation of many as Wholf's Tavern.

Evastus Livingston Morse purchased the Music Hall in the late 1890s. He then converted the building into a bathhouse with the additions of a swimming pool, mineral water baths, and a water bar. From this point forward, the building became known as the Music Hall Bathhouse Company. Included in his purchase of the Music Hall was a large tract of the surrounding land.

Evastus Morse began drilling on his newly acquired property near the end of North Main Street. Here he discovered the Salt Sulphur Water Spring in 1899. He pumped the water from this deep well directly into the pavilion at the Music Hall. The water from this spring was also later pumped into Harr's Pavilion on West Broadway Street and into the Salt Sulphur Pavilion at the Elms hotel. In 1937, the Salt Sulphur Spring was among the 10 pumped into the Hall of Waters.

Constructed in 1898, the Music Hall, pictured around 1900, held over 1,300 patrons. The building was located on Thompson Street facing west just northeast of the Elms hotel. In the late 1890s, the building was converted into a mineral water bathhouse with a swimming pool and water bar. (From the Missouri Valley Special Collections, Kansas City Public Library, Kansas City, Missouri.)

A military encampment just outside of Excelsior Springs was a regular fixture in the community. This photograph, taken in 1892, represents a small slice of life during that time. It has been stated that recruits for the Spanish-American War from this same encampment were being entertained at the Music Hall during the night just prior to May 9, 1898, when an early morning fire that destroyed the first Elms hotel broke out. (From the Missouri Valley Special Collections, Kansas City Public Library, Kansas City, Missouri.)

As with many haunted locations in Excelsior Springs, the stories of major traumatic events overlap and tie into each other. It was here at the Music Hall on the fateful night of May 9, 1898, that reports from the community place recruits for the Spanish-American War under the command of Capt. William Abernathy enjoying a relaxing break from training when the fire that destroyed the first Elms hotel broke out.

Nothing further has been revealed, but perhaps these recruits rushed from the Music Hall to the fire at the Elms to aid in extinguishing the flames. This could only have occurred if the recruits were at a late-night performance on May 8 and stayed in the area, since most documents point to the fire occurring in the early morning hours. But if the recruits were on hand, it may help to explain why, although the structure was wooden and highly susceptible to quickly being destroyed in a fire, not a single living soul was lost in the blaze.

A second Elms hotel opened in 1908. Sadly, 1908 was the same year that fire ravaged the Music Hall on September 24. This grand structure was never rebuilt. Stories surrounding the ghostly activity in the area seem to be more on the scale of urban legend. Only rumors passed on by others tell of the sounds of operatic music drifting into the air. However, several employees at the Elms Resort have reported the sounds of an opera singer inside of the Grand Ballroom late at night. Perhaps these related incidents may help to substantiate the rumors of operatic melodies still lingering in the atmosphere.

Redmond's Furniture

Kim Watson and Cindy Hamilton, sisters and co-owners of Redmond's Furniture, have fond memories of visiting the former Flanders's Department Store as children. This majestic three-story redbrick building in the heart of the historic shopping district of Excelsior Springs was constructed between 1900 and 1905. The outline of the words "FLANDERS DEPT STORE" can still be seen just below the second-story windows. Guests to Redmond's Furniture still cross the original entrance, where the floor displays white and green tiles in a decorative geometric pattern with the word "Flanders" clearly spelled out in front of each entry door.

When Flanders was constructed, the original owner was C.E. Flanders. He was also the owner of the Relief Springs Hotel from 1901 until 1904 and operated the luxury hotel and bath resort under the name of the Marietta Hotel. The property was located near the basin of Dry Fork of the Fishing River on North Marietta and Caldwell Streets.

When he sold the property in 1904 to C.C. Carter for $11,500, he also received what would soon become the home of Flanders Dry Goods Store property. Together with his wife, Ella Jean Flanders, the business became highly successful throughout the years. Over time, daughter Lorraine Hinn followed their example and took over management of the company. Lorraine Hinn was fervently involved in the Excelsior Springs community; she served for many years on the Job Corps community relations board and was a charter member of the Excelsior Springs Museum.

Kim Watson and Cindy Hamilton chose to remain as true as possible true to the original floor plan of their historic property when resurrecting the downtown business. Visitors to Redmond's today enter a spacious two-story-high showroom with additional mezzanine shopping areas along the north and south walls. It is easy to notice the beautiful tin ceiling panels and original pulley system crisscrossing the ceiling. This antique pulley system was very handy during the many years the building served as Flanders Department Store.

Customers can easily discern after climbing the wide wooden staircase to the rear of the store that the display rooms on the third floor were once a series of small apartments. For over 70

The outline of the words "FLANDERS DEPT STORE" can still be seen below the second-story windows of this building, constructed in the 1900s. The original entrance walkway still displays white and green tiles with the word "Flanders" at the entry door. (Author's collection.)

years, the boardinghouse on the third level housed ailing patients and their families visiting Excelsior Springs for the medical clinics offering the curative mineral water treatments. Visitors pausing on the staircase can spy the original doorway, which once upon a time opened onto a covered walkway for the patients to travel directly from their rooms to the medical clinics and to the famous Hall of Waters for treatment. It may be that the long history of this floor is the reason that Redmond's Furniture is a hot spot for ghostly activity. Kim and Cindy and several members of the staff have experienced multiple encounters with the paranormal.

As the following stories will demonstrate, the ghosts of Redmond's Furniture can make their presences known at any time of the day or night and under any circumstance. For the paranormal traveler, this store offers the rare and unique opportunity of a high probability of bumping into one of the many invisible inhabitants.

It was on a beautiful spring morning that Joni, a full-time employee of Redmond's, experienced her first otherworldly encounter while on the job. She was working in the back of the store with another employee when they both heard a loud crashing sound near the front doors. With her heart beating quickly, Joni rushed across the showroom floor towards the source of the disruption until she spied a large pile of women's purses on the floor. Only a few minutes earlier, these purses were neatly arranged on top of a display unit of metal shelves; now they were heaped in a pile at her feet near the bottom of the shelves. Oddly enough, the purses on the two remaining shelves below were completely undisturbed. Since a bell rings when guests enter, Joni was certain no one had entered the store. She remarks, "It was if an unseen hand in one quick push shoved all the purses from the top shelf." The display rack has since been moved to the back of the showroom in the attempt to dissuade the ghosts from creating any additional disturbances with the purses.

Another occasion that is remembered by several employees occurred during a busy fall afternoon, a day when Redmond's was bustling with holiday shoppers. A female customer had just spent a considerable amount of time on the third floor. She pushed past customers waiting at the front counter register and abruptly interrupted Cindy in mid-sale. Out of breath and speaking quickly, the customer loudly queried, "Do you know you have friends here?"

"Oh, you mean the ghosts," Cindy replied while trying to be as polite as possible given the awkward situation.

"Yes, but they're friendly," the customer hurriedly remarked before quickly exiting the store.

It is unknown how many desperately ill patients, seeking a miracle cure, made the boardinghouse apartments their last stop on the way to the other realm, but employees at Redmond's frequently hear footsteps and muffled sounds of conversations emanating from the third-floor areas. Ever attentive to their customers' needs, employees are accustomed to traveling up the long flight of stairs only to find themselves alone on the third floor. It does not take long to realize that they have been fooled by the ghosts of Redmond's once again.

Patrons discovering the third floor are instantly amazed at the superior decorating skills of owners Cindy and Kim, for every room on this floor is filled with expert groupings of picturesque examples of their work. The floor also clearly showcases details from the building's historic past. Swinging wooden doorways, brass apartment numbers, original bathrooms, wide wooden floorboards, and exposed original brick are just a few of the unique touches that heighten the shopper's experience of stepping into the past. But even in the midst of this beauty, Melissa, another employee at Redmond's, relates the following episode to explain the reason she no longer wishes to work on the third floor alone.

On this particular day, Melissa had kept herself busy all afternoon dusting the vast amounts of furniture, tables, decorating accents, and artwork displays on the third floor. She had worked her way slowly and silently, beginning near the top of the stairway on the east side of the building and was now working on the rooms toward the west. A soft shaft of light from the afternoon sun filtered in through the window, illuminating the room where she was working and making the dust easy to find. This particular room was decorated in a masterful display of bronze, leather, dark wood, and majestic tan hues, all in perfect harmony. The only color appearing out of place was the pale blue of Melissa's flittering dust rag.

After dusting a russet-colored chaise lounge, Melissa set her blue rag down for just a moment and crossed the room to replace a small picture frame that had fallen over on an end table near the window. When she turned back around to resume dusting, her dust cloth was nowhere in sight. Melissa quickly checked her pockets, peered underneath the chaise lounge, and then continued on searching the entire room but to no avail. She even went so far as to look for the dust cloth in the adjoining rooms. After a thorough search, Melissa went down the hallway to get some tissue paper from the bathroom to continue her dusting. When she returned to the room where she had last been working, there in the middle of the chaise lounge, plain as day, was the pale blue dust cloth.

Co-owner Kim Watson also shares a ghostly encounter she experienced in broad daylight while working on the third floor. She was walking out of one of the many display rooms and was rounding the corner to enter an adjacent hallway, when out of the corner of her eye she spied a small boy sitting quietly in a chair at a dining table near the center of the room. When Kim glanced back over her shoulder, the boy had completely vanished. Kim assumed the child's parents must be browsing nearby with the child in tow, so she continued on down the hall. Quickly Kim checked around for the child's parents, only to discover that she was entirely alone on the third floor. Even though this encounter lasted for a brief moment, she still has a clear picture of the child etched permanently into her memory. She describes him as young, probably about eight or nine years old, wearing a faded tan buttoned-up shirt and sporting a pageboy haircut with light brown hair. Perhaps this child is the same entity who played the trick on Melissa with the dust rag.

During the winter of 2008, when festive Christmas trees and a huge assortment of fun holiday decorations adorned every available inch of the main floor and the mezzanine levels at Redmond's Furniture, a bizarre series of paranormal events began to unfold.

It all began near the end of a typical business day while Cindy Hamilton talked to a customer at the front counter. Standing behind this counter, Cindy had a very clear view of the Christmas trees and ornaments on display near the back of the showroom floor. In one quick moment, a white birdhouse decoration flew off a tree. It traveled nearly six feet in the air in a straight line away from the tree before falling down onto the floor and landing quietly face up. Rarely unnerved by the little ghostly events at her store, Cindy picked up the object and returned the ornament to its rightful place amidst a tree decorated in soft whites and simmering with accents of silver. Without further thought of the ornament, she continued on with her work and finished out her day.

Less than a week later, the employees of Redmond's were gathered in the office eating lunch when all of a sudden they heard a loud thump out on the sales floor. In a group, they hurried out to see what had caused the strange sound. Imagine their surprise when they discovered, once again, that same small white birdhouse ornament six feet from its tree and once again laying face up, unharmed on the floor.

Yet another eerie event occurred just two days later. A new tree had been added to the large holiday collection on the main floor in honor of Kim's birthday. Done up in the usual grand manner of a major birthday event, this tree was adorned with black ribbons and round black glass ornaments. It stood only five feet high but appeared much larger after Redmond's employees placed it on top of a display table in the very center of the showroom floor.

Cindy and her sister Kim were telling a customer about the rather unusual and quite possibly ghostly events of the past few days and the frequent flights of the birdhouse ornament when the ghost made its presence known once again. One of the delicate black glass bulbs came off of the birthday tree. Amazingly, the ornament missed crashing on the table beneath and avoided smashing onto the floor below, but it did manage to roll gently across the floor nearly 10 feet until it came to a stop. As fate would have it, Susan, the only employee who up until this point had never experienced a paranormal event and according to other employees was the least likely to ever believe in the supernatural, was the first one to witness the movement of the bulb. Susan let out a yelp that attracted the attention of Cindy, Kim, and their customer. It is a rare event when a ghost makes an appearance by moving objects in front of multiple witnesses in broad daylight, but at Redmond's these events seem to continue to occur on a regular basis.

Cindy and Kim leave visitors with this final tale given to them by the previous owner of Redmond's Furniture. The owner often worked late into the night, buried in paperwork and details, but she always made it a habit not to stay too late. The ghosts of Redmond's have their own way of letting visitors and owners alike know that when it gets late into the evening, it is now the ghosts' time to take possession of their home. Anyone remaining past the midnight hour will become overwhelmed by the desire of the deceased residents at Redmond's to have the living leave the building—and leave quickly.

Redmond's Furniture
107 W. Broadway Street
Excelsior Springs, MO 64024
Hours of Operation:
Monday–Saturday
10:00 a.m.–5:00 p.m.
Phone: (816) 630-9100
www.RedmondsAtHome.com

Lithia No. 1, discovered around 1884, was originally a private water supply. A small pagoda located at 247 East Broadway was labeled, "Lithia—Willow Park." It contained a small hand pump for visitors to use. (From the private collection of Jim and Daphne Bowman.)

After analysis of the chemicals in the water, a large pavilion with a stone archway was constructed at 245 East Broadway Street. This entryway to the spring, seen in a 1930s postcard, was directly west of the building that currently houses the Willow Spring Mercantile. (From the private collection of Jim Masson.)

Four

HAUNTED RESTAURANTS

BLUE BIRD BISTRO AND WILLOW SPRING MERCANTILE

Jim and Daphne Bowman chose a historic location in downtown Excelsior Springs to realize their dream of running their own business. After falling in love with the over-100-year-old building, signing the papers, and renovating this distinctive part of the city's past, they were unaware that as owners of Willow Spring Mercantile their new job description would include playing host to a spirit from the past.

Stepping into Willow Spring Mercantile is one of the quickest ways to experience a step directly into the past of Excelsior Springs. The shop has the look and feel of a local 19th-century dry goods establishment. After renovations, its shop featured wide-planked hardwood floors, natural soft lighting, and high ceilings. The owners have wisely added country-scented candles to their mix of merchandise to further re-create an atmosphere of days gone by for all the senses.

Perhaps it is the accuracy of Jim and Daphne in re-creating a shop of the past that has helped the ghost of Willow Spring Mercantile to hang on into the present. This spirit may be visiting the familiar sights, sounds, and smells that were prevalent in the early years of Excelsior Springs, for the ghost at 249 East Broadway Street would appear to be that of a frequent customer of long ago. Often, when no one is near or the staff at Willow Springs is busy elsewhere, such as working in the back or serving delicious meals and pouring wine downstairs at the bistro, the old cow bell over the front door will clearly ring, and the sound of footsteps creaking across the wooden floor will announce that a customer has entered the store. Owner Daphne related:

> All of us have at one time or another come up the stairs to the sound of the bell and footsteps to find the store completely empty. But it isn't frightening or disturbing; there is nothing uncomfortable about the ghost's visits to our store. Once in a great while there will be a small item left on the countertop by the register. It's as if something or someone wishes to buy it and simply can't.

Upon researching this location, the owners were kind enough to point out that Willow Spring Mercantile stands directly to the east of what was once the entrance to Lithia No. 1 Spring. With their love of the past, Jim and Daphne have created a relaxing terrace garden and gazebo on the empty hillside where visitors once thronged to the healing spring.

Excelsior Springs: Haunted Haven

Research has uncovered that Lithia No. 1 was discovered in either 1883 or 1884 by Thomas McCullin and was originally a private water supply. As documented in the publication *Excelsior Springs, America's Haven of Health*, a small pagoda located at 247 East Broadway Street was labeled "Lithia—Willow Park." It contained a small hand pump for visitors to partake of the waters. After an analysis of the chemical contents in the water of the spring was released, a large pavilion with a distinctive stone archway was constructed at 245 East Broadway Street.

When visiting the Willow Spring Mercantile, please take the time to walk down the hillside on the original steps of Lithia No. 1. This short but scenic journey will help transform one's experience into the past and help gain a greater understanding of the ghosts lingering in Excelsior Springs.

An excerpt found on the Willow Spring Mercantile website, written by Daphne Bowman, explains the wonderful shopping and dining experience that awaits visitors to this historic location:

> Willow Spring Mercantile in beautiful Excelsior Springs, Missouri offers an array of quality products that are made in Missouri and around the Midwest. Jim and Daphne Bowman, their children Madi, Kennedy and Colt run the business. This team strives to provide you with exceptional products and service. Daphne & Jim offer friendly professional service and keep the sales floor full of an array of unique products. Jim creates and builds custom primitive and rustic furniture in the basement, and occasionally you can catch him on the sales floor playing guitar passing time. The kids are usually helping in the basement bistro or on the floor. After a couple of visits you will want to return because you always feel welcome and part of the family. The wine is always pouring and the coffee is always on . . .
>
> We strive to exceed our customer's expectations—we will do everything we can to meet your needs.

Willow Spring Mercantile
249 E Broadway Street
Excelsior Springs, MO 64024
Hours of Operation:
Tuesday–Friday, 10:00 a.m.–6:00 p.m.
Saturday, 10:00 a.m.–5:00 p.m.
Sunday, 12:00 p.m.–5:00 p.m.
(Sample wine all days they are open)
Contact: Jim and Daphne Bowman
Phone: (816) 630-SHOP (7467)
Fax: (816) 630-7467
shopthemercantile@yahoo.com
www.shopthemercantile.com

Ray's Diner

Established in 1932, Ray's Diner was built at the present location in 1947. It is undoubtedly one of the most active haunted locations in Excelsior Springs. It was my friend Shirley Griffin who first sat me down in a booth at Ray's Diner and told me to be ready to enjoy one of the best hamburgers of my life. Shirley had been busy gathering stories for this publication and knew the owners were happy to share not only their great food but also the tales of the ghost of Ray, the original owner.

This historical photograph of Lithia No. 1 is from the 1930s. The spring's unique stone archway can be seen peering above the line of Model-A Fords. (From the private collection of Jim and Daphne Bowman.)

This current photograph of Willow Spring Mercantile shows antique cars, giving a nostalgic touch to this historic location. (Author's collection.)

Ray's Diner can be seen as a small white building with the word "HAMBURGERS" written boldly above the windows on the left side of this 1930s street scene facing east down Broadway Street. The diner opened in 1932 across the street from its present location. (From the Atlas Bar Collection.)

The diner seats just 26 at two booths, two tables, eight counter stools, and when the weather is nice four outside tables. The atmosphere elicits a sense of nostalgia in this 1930s-style eatery. Pictures are everywhere, overwhelming one's mind as the aroma of grilled burgers and fries wafts through the air. And the chances of running into the former owner, Ray, or rather his ghostly appearance, are high.

Ghost hunters and curiosity seekers alike should stick around long enough for owner Ron Prewitt; his fast-cooking wife, Brenda; and speedy servers Stephanie and Natasha to get a minute to share their stories of the paranormal side of Ray's. Ron Prewitt is often mistaken for diner namesake Ray by visitors. He accepts this misnomer gracefully, seeing it as an opening to tell the tale of Ray's diner and its ghostly resident.

Ray opened his diner across the street from its present location in 1932 and ran his restaurant very successfully until 1955. The move to the southern side of the street in 1947 did not reduce the popularity of his cooking. In 1955, tragedy struck, with a terminal diagnosis of cancer from his doctor. Ray sold his beloved diner to someone who promised to keep his secret of success by continuing to run the diner same way Ray had all those years. Then Ray went home to put his affairs in order and live out the remaining days of his life. The diagnosis was grim; Ray was given only six months to live. One can easily imagine Ray's surprise and shock when his health did not decline. On a later visit to the doctor, he was given a completely clean bill of health. There was no sign of cancer in his system at all. Somehow a horrible mistake had been made; Ray did not and probably never did have cancer.

Ray was once again looking forward to a long and profitable life and rushed to buy back his diner. But one major obstacle stood in his path to reclaiming his former life: the new owners were not selling, not to Ray or anyone else. Sad and forlorn, Ray lived out the remainder of his life in Excelsior Springs watching the fruits of his labor become the success of another owner. Ray had to be content to visit his beloved diner, tell his tales of famous visitors of the past, and eat another guy's rendition of his famous chili recipe. "Almost as good, but not quite," he would tell the new owner. Yet today the recipe is still a closely guarded secret only the owners know. As current owner Ron tells it, "Ray was always disgruntled, disappointed that he couldn't go back into the diner to serve his customers again. He felt cheated by life and never quite recovered his happy disposition." Locals will say that they agree with that assessment, and perhaps that is why the ghost of Ray remains.

When entering Ray's Diner, take the time to carefully check out the pictures and articles from the past on the walls. Ron Prewitt states that many a customer has found the need to duck when the ghost of Ray rips the pictures and articles about himself off of the wall. The pictures and stories, still intact in their frames, are literally thrown by the ghost of Ray at customers. "We've gone through so many frames that I'm starting to buy them up at garage sales by the box-full," states Ron. He has returned one picture to the wall with the glass still broken as a testament to the frequent flying episodes. He says, "All we ask of Ray is that he doesn't hit any of the customers with the flying glass." Ray's escapades of throwing pictures appear to take place about six to seven times a year. They occur during business hours and seem to happen more often during the winter months and less frequently during the summertime.

Many faithful customers will gladly share their experiences with Ray's playful antics. Some admit to sensing someone sitting beside them on the counter stool, a movement of air, a brush of the arm, or a whiff of aftershave, but no one is there. Ray is generally seen as a ghostly apparition on the east side of the restaurant where the grill originally stood. He is seen wearing his familiar white chef's hat and apron, just as he did for over 20 years when he owned and ran the diner.

Ray's ghost likes to play games on the current staff at the diner. His favorite prank is to undo their work behind them. A coffee pot has been pulled off the coffee maker when no one was near. Ray's ghost has been known to repeatedly turn off a light that has just been turned on or visa versa.

Ron will quickly admit that he has a pet peeve about the backs of the bar stools being out of place. He always very carefully lines the stools up so that their backs are in a straight line every night before he leaves. The ghost of Ray has been known to turn all the chairs at the bar sideways during the night.

Some of the prankish happenings owners and the diners experience on an almost-daily basis seem to relate to former owner Ray's continual teasing nature. Others show a little more attitude toward the present occupants. Ray's ghost has been known to jerk the cooler door open, bonking Ron on the forehead. And the ghost has held the door to the cooler closed for no obvious reason, only to suddenly release it when Brenda least expects. "It gets annoying, but at least it is never boring at Ray's Lunch," says co-owner Brenda. "My worst experience with the ghost was seeing his shadow in the hallway on the bathroom door. It was nearly dark and the shadow was huge. I knew it was him by the double-pointed cook's hat he wore in all the pictures. So I said 'Ray, I'm going home for the night. Please don't leave a big mess for me to clean up in the morning!" Ron relates:

> Ray hates change! Whenever we move things around or try adding something different like a new light above the grill, Ray expresses his disapproval by knocking off the moved item or unplugging the lights or darkening some of the bulbs, along with the ever-present picture on the floor. That is kind of a standard reminder that it is still his diner and we are just the custodians of it.

Long-term employee Stephanie playfully refers to the ghost as "Ray the brat," as he is always teasing her with a moved order pad, a missing pen, or a cleaning rag moved from where it was left. "Ray doesn't like change," Stephanie informs customers and goes on to explain that she was witness when a mini-pinball machine scooted from where it was mounted on a high corner shelf and was dropped to the counter below. She gasps in telling her story, "I saw a white hand appear out of nowhere and place the machine in a gentle gesture back to where it originally sat for many years. We moved it down to a lower location after that, and it hasn't moved since."

On several occasions when employee Natasha has gone downstairs, she has heard loudly stomping footsteps overhead and the sound of slamming doors, often hard enough to vibrate knickknacks off the shelf. She has also heard the occasional burst of laughter off in the distance. Natasha calmly tells visitors, "I feel like I am never here alone, and sometimes that is comforting."

Both employees, Stephanie and Natasha, have heard footsteps across the floor when no one was around. They have been startled on several occasions by the sound of the restroom door down the hallway slamming shut apparently all by itself. Both of the women and several frequent customers have seen the ghost of Ray in the hallway as well.

Other sightings of Ray have been reported by local residents passing by the diner late at night. One story was given to me by Corky Barnett, a frequent customer of Ray's Diner. "It's a common sight to find the lights on and what looks like someone who is busy cleaning up around 2:00 to 3:00 a.m., when no one else is in the building. I have seen it several times myself. I have always called Ron the next morning. But Ron is always adamant that he was not in the diner at 2:00 a.m. the night before."

Ron joined in this conversation and informed everyone in the restaurant that it is always after a night when Ray has been seen walking about or cleaning in the building that Ron will come in the next morning to find many, if not all, of the bar stools turned in different directions. "Ray really makes a point of letting me know he's been here by changing the chairs, which is one thing that bugs me the most!"

The stark white exterior paint of this petite diner, pictured around the 1930s, helped it to stand out amid the larger surrounding buildings. Despite its small stature, this tiny operation was extremely successful. (From the private collection of Ron Prewitt.)

Ray's diner relocated to the southern side of Broadway Street in 1947. Ray is seen in this 1950s photograph sporting his familiar white chef's cap. (From the private collection of Ron Prewitt.)

If you plan to stop by Ray's Diner, remember the hours are from 7:00 a.m. until 2:00 p.m., serving a delicious breakfast and lunch. Many recommend the chili, served up hot by the bowl. And if you wish to question Ron or any of the staff about the ghost of Ray, the rule at Ray's Diner is patience. The food is so good that the diner is frequently packed, and the employees are very busy. Just wait your turn, and perhaps—just perhaps—Ray will throw a picture at you while you wait.

Ray's Diner
"Serving the community since 1932"
231 E. Broadway Street
Excelsior Springs, MO 64024
Phone: (816) 637-3432

VENTANA'S GOURMET GRILL

The building that houses Ventana's Gourmet Grill began as the Boston Store in the early 1900s. By 1917, the location was home to the J.D. Holmes Store, named for proprietor Jesse D. Holmes. This early store was a place for locals to shop for dry goods, ready-wear clothing, and hats. The store became J.D. Holmes and Son by 1925, although no records remain of Holmes and Son after 1926.

Ventana's Gourmet Grill, just a few doors west of Redmond's, is a great place to stop for a healthy breakfast or lunch. With French bistro flair, Ventana's offers gourmet food without the gourmet prices. After taking in the sight of the high tin-tiled ceilings, dark hardwood floors, and the classic ambiance of this location, one might have the feeling of being watched, for it has been discovered that Ventana's has two ghostly residents.

The current owners purchased this historic location in 2002. Ghostly activity was first discovered during the renovations by a little girl who was keeping herself entertained while her parents and grandparents worked to transform the empty building. She frequently talked to and about her imaginary friend. Upon questioning, her family discovered this imaginary friend was a little girl about the same age as their child, who seemed to be blessed with the gift of creating a make-believe universe. Her family was happy that the girl was well behaved and had an active imagination until they questioned her further about her "imaginary friend."

It was then that this living girl related the tale of her ghostly friend. She said the friend had broken her neck and died. In later retellings of the story, the tale of the demise of this unseen adolescent grew—this friend was pushed down a flight of stairs inside the building, thus causing her unfortunate death. It was this dark revelation from an innocent child that startled the family of entrepreneurs, because the back portion of the building had been previously sealed off, and the child had not been made aware of the existence of a hidden stairway leading to the second floor.

The two girls continued in their play until one day the living child announced that her friend could not come out and play with her any more. It seems the ghost child had a mean grandfather, the same person who had pushed her down the stairs. It was this grandfather that had forbidden the living little girl and the ghostly little girl to play together ever again. The older ghostly presence was upset that others, presumably the family of the living little girl, were now well aware of his haunting presence and the presence of his ghostly granddaughter.

Research has not yet revealed the identities of the mysterious ghosts of Ventana's Gourmet Grill, but evidence of a grizzly murder taking place on the sidewalk outside of this establishment

Still featuring its original high tin-tiled ceiling, Ventana's Gourmet Grill, on the southeast corner of Broadway and Marietta Streets, is a great place for breakfast or lunch. The building that houses Ventana's Gourmet Grill began in the early 1900s as the Boston Store and by 1917 was home to the J.D. Holmes Store. This store featured dry goods, ready-wear clothing, and hats. (Photograph by Joseph Kline.)

The building to the immediate left in this early-1900s photograph is a side view of the Boston Store. The picture focuses on the southeast corner of Broadway and Marietta Streets and is seen from Broadway facing south. On December 3, 1900, rivals Albert Chambers and Thomas McMullin crossed paths at this location—Chambers did not survive. (From the Atlas Bar collection.)

NIGHT SCENE, MARIETTA STREET, EXCELSIOR SPRINGS, MO.

This 1910s postcard sheds an eerie light on the spot where the two rivals met. Chambers was outside of the Boston Store headed west along Broadway Street. McMullin was heading north on the west side of Marietta Street toward the Boston Store. A shot rang out into the night. Chambers, bleeding from the chest, left in a southwest direction. McMullin pocketed a pistol and strolled away. Five days later, Chambers died. (From the Excelsior Springs Museum and Archives Collection.)

was provided by the Clay County Museum and Historical Society in nearby Liberty, Missouri. Early in the afternoon on December 3, 1900, two longtime rivals, Albert Chambers and Thomas McMullin, accidently crossed paths on the wintery street.

Chambers was walking outside of the Boston Store heading west along Broadway. At the same time, McMullin, accompanied by business acquaintance Samuel Rowell, was heading north on the west side of Marietta Street toward the Boston Store. At the corner, Rowell separated from McMullin and crossed Broadway, continuing north. As fate would have it, Chambers and McMullin passed each other on the sidewalk outside of the Boston Store. Someone swore at the other and a shot rang out. Chambers lifted his left hand to his bleeding chest, and then more slowly his trembling right hand covered the wound as well. He staggered off down the street away from McMullin in a southwest direction. At the same time, McMullin pocketed his pistol and strolled slowly up the street smoking a cigar. Both men later testified as to their own innocence (Chambers gave a death-bed statement), claiming not to be the instigator of this event and firmly blamed the incident on the other party.

Five days would pass before Chambers died from his chance meeting on the street. During this time, he gave multiple statements that he had done nothing to provoke the shooting. Later, during his trial for murder, McMullin testified that Chambers swore loudly, drew a knife, and approached him menacingly in an attempt to possibly stab him at close range. He claimed he shot Chambers in self-defense. Testimony was given by several witnesses; only one claimed to have seen a knife, but two others testified it had not been drawn. Thomas McMullin was found guilty of second-degree murder and sentenced to 20 years in prison.

Perhaps one day in the near future, a paranormal team might gather in the dining room at Ventana's on a December 3rd afternoon and attempt a conversation with this visitor from the past.

Ventana's Gourmet Grill
117 West Broadway Street
Excelsior Springs, MO 64024
Phone: (816) 630-8600
Hours of Operation:
Monday–Saturday
11:00 a.m.–8:30 p.m., serving lunch and dinner

WABASH BBQ

If the scent drifting by in the air is causing your mouth to water and your stomach to growl, there is a very good chance you are approaching the Wabash BBQ, home of Excelsior Springs' award-winning smoked barbecue. Located just south and practically in the shadow of the Elms Resort & Spa in the historic Wabash Railroad depot building, it is now a welcoming gathering place for locals and spirits alike.

Although the line of the Wabash Railroad leading into Excelsior Springs was only 8.7 miles long and lasted only a brief five years from 1927 until 1933, the line served a vital purpose in opening up the town to direct railroad traffic. The Wabash assisted in linking railroad traffic from Buffalo, St. Louis, and New York City in larger numbers than were possible in the past. The redbrick Mission-style structure was constructed on land that was previously home to the Excelsior Springs Riding Academy. Furthermore, the exact placement of the Wabash Depot is over the site of the horse barn that had been destroyed by a fire in May 1927.

Constructed in 1927 on the spot that was previously the Excelsior Springs Riding Academy, this redbrick Mission-style structure, seen in a 1930s postcard, was the railway depot for the Wabash line leading into Excelsior Springs. (From the Excelsior Springs Museum and Archives Collection.)

Taken en route, this late-1920s photograph is a side view of a Kansas City, Clay County & St. Joseph Railway car. The words "Excelsior Springs Route" can be seen labeled near the front and the back of the railcar. (From the Missouri Valley Special Collections, Kansas City Public Library, Kansas City, Missouri.)

Located inside the former Wabash Railroad depot building is the award-winning Wabash BBQ. It is located just south of the Elms. (Author's collection.)

This latest addition to the rails of Excelsior Springs was smaller than the grand Old Milwaukee Depot to the north. A dummy line ran between the two depots, helping to carry weary travelers from across the nation and even from around the world quickly to their hotel destinations so that they could partake of the healing waters nearby. And it would seem that two of these travelers who must have lingered just a little too long in the Wabash Depot have never left.

The staff was questioned, and one longtime employee by the name of Heather was brave enough to step forward and be interviewed about the ghosts of the Wabash. She sat on a bar stool in the southern half of the building next to the long antique wooden bar. There, in the early morning before working hours, she began relating her otherworldly experiences. She had a wide, bright smile and shoulder-length blond hair. Her voice and friendly manner were clear signs of why she is a superior waitress and a great hostess for the Wabash BBQ. Heather pointed to the northern portion of the restaurant.

The Wabash BBQ is clearly split into two halves that were constructed at different times to serve separate business purposes. The northern, or nonsmoking, side of the current restaurant was the original home of the Wabash Depot, and the southern portion, or smoking side, containing four rooms, was added several years later to house the Quality Milk Company. The Quality Milk Company produced dairy items and utilized the former depot section of the building as a restaurant. Over time, the restaurant closed, but under the later ownership of the Mid-America Dairy Association, the dairy operation remained successful for many years up until 1985.

The southern half contains the long, well-crafted wooden bar that originally served patrons for many years prior at the Elms Resort. It was assumed prior to this meeting that the ghosts of the Wabash BBQ were attached to the early history of this massive bar taken from the Elms, which is practically bursting at the seams with spirits of the past, but the stories place both entities of the Wabash clearly on the other side in the northern portion of the restaurant.

A keen eye visiting the nonsmoking section at the Wabash BBQ today can still easily perceive the location of the original railroad ticket window, baggage room, and waiting room area that once served thousands of guests. It is here in the former depot that the activities of two ghostly entities have been reported. The more active of the two ghosts is one that the owners and employees at the Wabash BBQ have jokingly named "John," because he most frequently makes his presence known in or near the public bathrooms. John will turn a light on or off almost immediately after an employee has flipped the light switch. As a general rule, though, John has been noticed far more frequently late at night when only one or two people are left doing the closing chores for the day. John repeatedly moves the cleaning supplies about, taking the them out of their carrier and placing them onto the floor nearby. Once in a rare while, John will unravel a toilet paper roll, sending the paper down the wall, across the floor, and out the door when no one else is around.

The menu at the Wabash BBQ comes complete with a history of the Wabash Railroad line in Excelsior Springs and Chillicothe, Missouri. Both historic railroad locations are now home to Wabash BBQ restaurants. The following is a brief excerpt from the menu:

Two lifetime Excelsior Springs residents saw the depot and visualized a longtime dream— to operate a restaurant. In February 1997, Jim and Cheri McCullough purchased the building and began renovating the old depot into the Wabash BBQ.

In between the two halves of the Excelsior Springs Wabash BBQ is a long, narrow kitchen. When current owners Jim and Cheri took one of their first pictures in this area, Cheri was holding the camera and Jim was standing next to their new cook. When the film was developed, both were amazed to find three people clearly in the picture. Was the third person in the picture John the ghost?

EXCELSIOR SPRINGS: HAUNTED HAVEN

The Old Milwaukee Depot no longer stands, but the empty site along the railroad tracks in northern Excelsior Springs bears investigation. Could it be that John still rides the long-defunct rails, disturbing the living on the hillsides along the way? Or John may be a former employee of the Wabash Railroad and is the ghost of both the Excelsior Springs and the Chillicothe Wabash BBQ's locations. This possibly unique anomaly deserves greater investigation, perhaps by future paranormal investigators.

Another entity that haunts the Wabash BBQ is a little girl. Very little is known about her, and she makes her appearance far less frequently than John the bathroom ghost. Employees of the Wabash have dubbed her "Laura" and sense that she may be the ghost of a five-year-old girl. There have only been a few rare occasions where the laughter of a little girl has been heard in north area. When this has occurred, no one was in the north side of the restaurant at all, but the giggling voice of a little girl carried over to be heard by the staff on the southern half.

Here is the one clear rule to obey when visiting the Wabash BBQ: please do not ask Ron the cook about spirit entities. He has been the driving force behind that wonderful flavor at the Wabash for many years but does not want to talk about or even know about the ghosts! So please, leave him be and continue to enjoy the great barbecue flavor at the Wabash on future visits.

Wabash BBQ
646 S. Kansas City Avenue
Excelsior Springs, MO 64024
Contact: Cheri McCullough
Phone: (816) 630-7700
Fax: (816) 630-7722
cheri@wabashbbq.com
www.wabashbbq.com

Five

A Spring on Every Corner

Excelsior Springs Mineral Water Springs and Wells

According to Troy Taylor in *The Ghost Hunter's Guidebook*:

> Many researchers have long believed that water and ghosts are inextricably tied together. Water is not only a conductor of electricity, in the case of homeopathic remedies it manages to retain a "memory" of the medicines that have been introduced to it. Could hauntings and water work the same way? Can tragic events leave behind a "memory" in the water of certain locations, replaying them over and over again like a recording? It's possible that this may be the reason why places that are infused with water are also so active when it comes to local ghosts.

From its conception with the discovery of Siloam Spring, at least 40 springs in Excelsior Springs carried four distinct types of mineral water: soda bicarbonate, iron manganese, saline sulphur, and calcium bicarbonate. The following list of mineral water springs and pavilions has been compiled from multiple sources. Many of the springs changed their names as the city progressed and when they had changes in ownership. An attempt has been made to include as many details and names of these locations as possible, which resulted in some locations being listed more than once under different names. This is not a complete guide but an honest attempt to sort through some of the multitude of overlapping information.

Very little is known about the well at 508 St. Louis Avenue other than it was one of many local locations that sold mineral waters.

The Blue Rock Lithia Well was known for producing the largest amounts of water. It was located on Seybold Road. This spring was also referred to as the Old Smith Spring. The well's calcium water was piped to the White Sulphur Pavilion at 505 Elms Boulevard behind the former post office on Isley Boulevard. The water was also sold at the Salt Sulphur Pavilion at 204 West Broadway Street.

Excelsior Springs: Haunted Haven

The Bottling Works facility was located on the west bank of the Fishing River near Regent Springs on South Kansas City Avenue. It processed many of the waters in the area, including Soterian Water, Soterian Ginger Ale, Regent, Siloam, and Sulpho Saline. No longer in existence, this structure sat just south of the Elms Resort & Spa Carriage House and across the street from the current location of the Wabash BBQ.

On the southeast corner of Saratoga Street and Benton Avenue, the Crystal Lithium Spring & Pavilion served calcium water. This spring supplied the Lithia Bottling Company on Beacon Hill. The bottling company produced soda and seltzer waters along with sarsaparilla and ginger ale.

The Elms Park Sulpho-Saline Pavilion was in the vicinity of the Mill Inn Restaurant on St. Louis Avenue.

Providing mild soda waters, the Empire Twin Wells were located south of the Elms Resort along the banks of Fishing River. It appears that these springs were renamed the Regent Spring and the Soterian Spring. Additional details are provided under Regent Spring and the Soterian Spring.

Not to be confused with the Excelsior Springs Lithia Spring, the site of the Excelsior Lithia Well can still be seen at 302 West Excelsior Street. A plaque reads, "Excelsior Lithia Well, Donated by Optimist Club Commerce Bank." This well has been filled in with concrete, but visitors can still see the original pump handle where travelers to Excelsior Springs lined up to partake of its healing waters.

The Excelsior Salt Saline Well was one of two wells located in a building on the current Community Center parking lot in the 200 block of South Thompson Avenue.

The Excelsior Soda Spring, at 401 East Excelsior Street, was better known as the Hiawatha Well, for it served guests at the Hiawatha Hotel.

The Excelsior Spring was the second spring opened to the pubic and was promoted as being 150 feet east of Siloam Spring. It was listed as one of the six original iron springs in the area. After brick buildings were erected along the neighboring street, the water was pumped from the basement of 219 East Broadway Street.

The Excelsior Springs Lithia Spring was a calcium water spring discovered in 1888 on the corner of East Broadway and Elizabeth Streets. It was located inside the Planters Hotel, and its waters were available on tap in the lobby. The Planters Hotel, which was directly north of the Siloam Spring, later became the Montezuma Bath House. The spring was renamed the Montezuma Lithia Spring.

Fowler's Magniferro Spring produced iron manganese water. It was found on the corner of North Marietta and West Excelsior Streets on the lawn of the Fowler Cottage. It was only feet from the Excelsior Lithia Well. Also under a hundred yards away and directly to the north, across the waters of the Dry Fork Branch of the Fishing River, was the site of the Relief Spring Hotel and Bath House.

Grant Well, also known as Soda Carbonic Spring, was located at the east end of Broadway Street.

Harr's Pavilion, once located at 206 West Broadway Street, provided salt sulphur water from the well near the end of North Main Street, white sulphur water drawn from well at 505 Elms Boulevard, and Blue Rock Lithia water from out on Seybold Road.

The Hiawatha Well was located at 401 East Excelsior Street. This spring is also listed in some documents as the Excelsior Soda Spring. Here, water was available from a hand pump atop a concrete slab. The well served guests at the nearby Hiawatha Boarding House, which was built as a two-and-a-half-story Queen Anne home in 1907.

At 406-408 Isley Boulevard stood Deep Hollow Cottage, owned by C.A. Hartshorn. This location was also the home of the Imperial Lithia Well (spring). The well's mineral waters were listed among the 16 lithia and neutral waters (calcium) of Excelsior Springs in the 2003 publication of *The Waters of Excelsior Springs, Valley of Vitality.*

The Bottling Works was located on the banks of the Fishing River just south of the Elms Resort. This facility processed many mineral waters from the area. (From the private collection of Betty Bissell.)

EXCELSIOR SPRINGS: HAUNTED HAVEN

Thomas Walker Jones had been the pump man at Siloam Spring for many years. The knowledge gained from this job served him well when he opened Jones Soda Well to the public in a small pavilion just outside his home at 421 East Excelsior Street. The well, drilled to 110 feet, soon became one of the most popular soda wells, even though its location was the furthest for travelers to visit on East Excelsior Street.

The Keystone Lithia Spring was the second well located in a building on the current Community Center parking lot in the 200 block of South Thompson Avenue. Formerly known as the Salt Sea Springs, Keystone Lithia was one of 10 waters that were later piped directly into the Hall of Waters.

The Link Soda Pavilion was at 200 East Excelsior Street near the corner of East Excelsior and Elizabeth Streets. This location also served saline water. The building was destroyed, but visitors can still stand inside the remains of the stone gazebo at the base of the hill that at one time was dominated by the view of Castle Rock Hotel. Cut into the wall directly to the north of the gazebo, the sealed-off entryways can still be seen today. The pavilion is also listed as Sulfo Salt or Sulphur-Salt Pavilion.

Lithia No. 1 (Spring) Well was located at 245 East Broadway Street (see page 110) and was discovered in either 1883 or 1884. It was used as the McMullin family water supply until its mineral properties were ascertained. A large stone pavilion with an attractive archway was constructed directly west of the former site of the Willow Park Lithia Spring. Additional information regarding the ghosts of Willow Spring Mercantile, located directly to the east of this property, can be found in chapter four of this publication.

The Lithiated Soda Well, a calcium water well, was owned by Sallie Callerman. It was drilled to a depth of 195 feet. Located at 302 West Excelsior Street, it was also known as Lithiated Soda Spring or the Soda Saline Well.

The Lithium Magnesium Spring was at 334 Foley Street along with the Seltzer Salt Soda Spring. The water from the spring was recommended for stomach, kidney, and intestinal problems.

Maurer's Salt Well was on the corner of the swimming pool at the Lake Maurer complex. The Lake Maurer summer resort was one mile south of Excelsior Springs. It was promoted as having the only outdoor resort with a mineral water swimming pool.

The McCleary Thornton–Minor Hospital, at 402 St. Louis Avenue, was constructed in 1927. The main focus of this facility was the spring waters and their healing powers. The water from the McCleary's Salt Well, located on the property, had such a high salt level that it was transformed into crystals and sold for use in bathwater.

The Mee Lithia Spring was located just west of the Saratoga Hotel at 204 East Excelsior Street.

Listed as containing soda bicarbonate waters, the Natrona Soda Spring was discovered at a depth of 111 feet at 402 East Excelsior Street. A pavilion for this well was originally reached by steps from Excelsior Street. John W. and Byrdie Cazzell later built a pavilion on the corner, increasing the popularity of this spring.

Old Smith Spring, located on Seybold Road, was known for producing the largest amounts of water. This spring was also referred to as the Blue Rock Lithia Well.

The Park Spring and Well, located in the Fishing River Linear Park, provided most of the lithia water dispensed at the Hall of Waters Water Bar. This location is also referred to as Park Lithia Spring.

The Peerless Water Company (Peerless Lithia Springs) was at 203 East Excelsior Street; its pavilion sold soda water.

Drilled to a depth of 45 feet, Pioneer Well is listed as containing soda bicarbonate water. The Pioneer Well was located next to the Mitchell Hotel on the 100 Block of South Street.

Regent Spring, an iron manganese spring, was discovered in 1881 and named the Empire Spring by Captain Farris, an attorney from Richmond. The spring was later renamed the

Regent
Springs
Excelsior
Springs, Mo.

J. S. KNIGHT,
Kansas City, Mo

The Regent Spring, originally named the Empire Spring, is seen in this 1900s postcard. It was just south of the Elms alongside of the Soterian Spring. (From the private collection of Betty Bissell.)

Siloam Spring was the very first mineral water spring in Excelsior Springs and was originally known as the Excelsior. On a regular basis, tourists would stop to have their picture taken as a keepsake of their journey. This group had their photograph taken around the 1890s. (From the private collection of Betty Bissell.)

SILOAM SPRING - EXCELSIOR SPGS, MO.   DURHAM '18.

Designed in 1917, the Siloam Spring Pavilion, pictured around the 1930s, stood side by side with the Sulpho-Saline Pavilion. Both ornate buildings were part of a larger complex by landscape architect George E. Kessler and architect Henry F. Hoit. (From the private collection of Betty Bissell.)

Regent Spring. It was just south of the Elms hotel across the Fishing River in Regent Park and alongside of the Soterian Spring. The pavilion for this spring could be accessed from the southwest corner of South Marietta and Richmond Streets. The waters from the Regent Spring were one of 10 that were piped directly into the Hall of Waters. The waters received a medal at the 1893 World's Fair in Chicago, which resulted in a great amount of publicity for Excelsior Springs.

Relief Spring was listed as the third mineral water spring discovered in the area. It was located near the basin of Dry Fork of the Fishing River on North Marietta Street and Caldwell Avenue and produced lithia water. It was reported that steel objects left in the basin overnight would obtain magnetic properties. Additional information is provided in the section titled, "Hope Residence and Relief Springs."

Salax Well was located in a shaft adjacent to the Relief Spring near North Marietta and Caldwell Streets but at a different depth. The Salax and Relief Springs had stone pavilions to help them weather the frequent flooding of the Dry Fork.

Salt Sea Springs was the second well located in a building on the current Community Center parking lot on the 200 block of South Thompson Avenue. Also known later as the Keystone Lithia Spring, it was one of 10 waters that were piped directly into the Hall of Waters. This spring has also been found listed as Excelsior Saline Spring and Salt Sea Excelsior Spring. The Salt-Sea Group was also located on South Thompson Avenue.

The Salt-Sulphur Booth was the pavilion on the property of a 900-foot-deep well on North Main Street.

Discovered in 1888, the water from the deep well at the end of North Main Street and Kennedy Avenue known as the Salt Sulphur Spring and Well was first pumped to several locations. Since the Salt Sulphur Spring and Well sat on the grounds of the Music Hall, the waters were pumped into the pavilion inside the hall on Thompson Avenue. These waters were also pumped to Harr's Pavilion on West Broadway Street and to the Salt Sulphur Pavilion at the Elms. Slat Sulphur was sold as a laxative and an aid to all stomach ailments at the cost of 1¢ per glass or 10¢ per gallon. The waters from the Salt Sulphur Spring and Well were one of the 10 mineral waters pumped directly into the Hall of Waters.

Saratoga Spring produced lithia water. Discovered at the corner of the Maples apartment building, its water was pumped and sold through a pavilion nearby on East Broadway Street. The water from the Saratoga Spring was considered to be relaxing in nature and was therefore nicknamed "Sleepy Water" by visitors to the spring.

The Seltzer Salt-Soda Spring, discovered by Jacob W. and Mrs. Samyra Wade Stollings in 1906 at 334 Foley Street, was drilled to a depth of 105 feet and produced soda water.

Producing iron manganese water, Siloam Spring was originally known as the Excelsior. It was the very first mineral water spring in Excelsior Springs discovered to have healing properties. This spring was home to an ornate pavilion along with the Sulpho-Saline Pavilion. Both buildings were part of the elaborate Siloam Gardens designed by landscape architect George E. Kessler and architect Henry F. Hoit. It is presently located under the north steps of the Hall of Waters on Broadway Street.

Located at the rear of Grant's Hotel, the Soda-Carbonic Spring at 424 East Broadway Street also was known by the name of Grant's Spring. It was listed among the soda bicarbonate waters along with 12 other springs in the city.

The Soda Saline Well, at 302 West Excelsior Street, was also referred to as Lithiated Soda Spring (or Well).

The Soterian Well was directly south of the Elms and just north of the Regent Spring. The Regent Spring was originally called the Empire Spring. Lithia waters from this well were later bottled in large quantities and shipped throughout the world.

Seven saline laxative springs were in Excelsior Springs, including the Sulpho-Saline Well, pictured around the 1890s, on North Main Street. Its waters were originally piped to pavilions on Broadway Street and in Elms Park. (From the private collection of Betty Bissell.)

This 1920s picture postcard, taken 30 years later, shows a group of visitors waiting near the Sulpho-Saline Pavilion and emphasizes the rapid growth of the city of Excelsior Springs. (From the private collection of Betty Bissell.)

This two-story circular stone-and-concrete well was constructed in 1912 to supply visitors with the iron manganese water from the Superior Springs. It still stands, although out of service, just south of Roosevelt Avenue in the Fishing River Linear Park. (Author's collection.)

EXCELSIOR SPRINGS: HAUNTED HAVEN

Steck's Iron Spring was just southwest of the Royal Hotel on Thompson Avenue. The spring was the property of Prof. W.E. Steck and was unavailable to the public until the city arranged with Professor Steck to construct a pagoda around the spring as well as a small park.

The waters of the Sulpho-Saline Well and Pavilion were one of seven saline laxative springs in Excelsior Springs. This 1,460-foot-deep well was found at the end of North Main Street. Originally its waters were piped to pavilions on Broadway Street and in Elms Park. The Sulpho-Saline Pavilion and the Siloam Pavilion were two ornate structures on the grounds of what is currently the Hall of Waters. Additional historical details are found in chapter three.

The Sulphur-Salt Pavilion building at 200 West Broadway Street was also known as the Link Soda Pavilion and Spring and sold waters from the Sulphur Salt-Soda Spring. The confusion comes from the sign across the top of the building, which read in bold letters, "LINK'S SODA AND SULFO SALT." Additional details can be found on page 104.

The Sulphur Salt-Soda Spring, owned by Miss M. Bierman, was discovered at a depth of 126 feet. This saline well was directly to the north of Relief Spring on Caldwell Street. The waters were promoted as a general tonic and were offered to the public for free for the first few months of its existence.

Sunnyside (Park Spring) was in the park on North Kansas City Avenue.

The iron manganese waters from Superior Springs Wells and Pagoda (Superior No. 1 and Superior No. 2 Springs) were available at the pagoda, which still stands just south of Roosevelt Avenue in the Fishing River Linear Park. The original wooden structure was built in 1901 and rebuilt in 1912 as a two-story circular stone and concrete well enclosure with a cone-shaped, wood-shingle room supported by four octagonal pillars. This structure still stands and is accessible for viewing.

The spring of the Vichy Group provided iodide soda water and could be found on East Excelsior Street near Elizabeth Street.

The water from White Sulphur Spring was one of 10 types pumped into the Hall of Waters for its swimming pool. The well is was located at 505 Elms Boulevard behind the large building that was once the post office and is now the Church of Christ on Isley Boulevard. Water from the Blue Rock Lithia Well was also sold at this location.

An early spring, Willow Park Lithia Spring, and its small pagoda were located at 247 East Broadway Street. The facility was later replaced by Lithia No. 1 at 245 East Broadway, featuring an attractive walk-through pavilion with a stone archway entrance. These facilities were located directly to the west of the current-day Willow Spring Mercantile and Blue Bird Bistro.

Six

AROUND EXCELSIOR SPRINGS

EXCELSIOR SPRINGS GOLF COURSE

According to Troy Taylor in *The Haunting Of America*:

> There are few places on the American landscape more haunted than Civil War battlefields, locations of violence, death, tragedy and bloodshed. In scores of these now empty fields, the conflict of war still plays out in the form of hauntings. These horrific re-enactments are recalled as not only the lost souls of men whose lives ended too soon, but gut-wrenching repetitions of memories imprinted on the atmosphere of places where so many lives were lost. War has left an indelible impression of the roads, fields, woods and homes of historic America.

Nearly lost to the annuals of history, the location of the Battle of Fredericksburg, Missouri, can be found on what are now the grassy rolling hills of the Excelsior Springs Golf Course on the southeast edge of Excelsior Springs. A small unassuming stone with a brass marker dedicated to those who lost their lives during the battle can be found near the 15th tee. It was near this location that the small hamlet of Fredericksburg once stood. The town and much of its history have long since been swallowed up by the expansion of the larger city of Excelsior Springs to the north.

The story of this brief skirmish on this land and the small log cabin that still exists inside of the Excelsior Springs Golf Course Club House are forever intertwined. Constructed in 1825, this cabin consisted mainly of walnut logs cut from the land and was the home of Edwin and Lettis O'Dell. Built a mere three years after the James family farm in nearby Kearney, the O'Dell cabin is one of the oldest structures within Clay County, Missouri. In 1830, Edwin obtained a patent for the 160-acre family farm. Over the years, this tiny cabin, with only one main room of 17 by 19 feet and a small sleeping loft above, became home to the O'Dells and their 10 children as well.

Lettis (Clevenger) O'Dell was the daughter of Richard and Sarah (Wood) Clevenger. Richard, along with brothers Samuel and Jesse, was among the first settlers of Ray County, coming with

The small cabin of Edwin and Lettis O'Dell, built in 1825, still exists inside of the Excelsior Springs Golf Course Club House. Built three years after the James family farm, the O'Dell cabin is one of the oldest remaining structures in Clay County, Missouri. (From the private collection of Betty Bissell.)

the O'Dells and others from Cocke County, Tennessee. Most were members of the Big Pigeon Baptist Church in Cocke County. Their extensive family tree was published in 1991 as the *Clevenger Families of Ray County, Missouri.*

Richard Clevenger, Lettis's father, was born around 1773 in Virginia. He was the son of Thomas & Psyche (Pittman) Clevenger and arrived in Ray County, Missouri, in 1818 or 1819. He was married to Sarah Wood in 1795 in Shenandoah, Virginia. They brought with them to Ray County their seven children: John, Lettis, Nancy, William Andrew, Rachel, Pitman, and Moses.

By the 1850s, Jesse O'Dell, one of the five sons of Edwin and Lettis, and his wife, Henrietta, were living in the cabin home and running the family farm. Over the previous 30 years, much of the timber had been cleared for pasture, and life had been peaceful with occasional visits from the local Osage Indians. Everything began to change with the encroachments of the Civil War in the early 1860s. Guerrilla warfare became commonplace in the area, and it may be that reports of the attack on the James farm during the summer of 1863 had reached the nearby community of Fredericksburg and the O'Dells. Additional details of the attack on the home of Jesse James and his family can be found in the following section and are eerily reminiscent of the events that took place at the O'Dell home prior to the Battle of Fredericksburg.

The Civil War came to the O'Dell family farm during the night of April 17, 1864. Guerrilla fighters found Jesse O'Dell outside the tiny cabin and began beating him. Inside the cabin, a very terrified and very expectant Henrietta O'Dell remained in hiding. After the soldiers were gone, Jesse found his wife safe inside but in premature labor. That very same night, in the loft above, Henrietta gave birth to a son. They named their small boy Edwin after his grandfather. The outlook was grim, and newborn Edwin was not expected to survive for long. Fortunately, he pulled through and many years later married twice and fathered 15 children. It is possible that this horrific incident left an impression inside the walls of the tiny farmhouse and may also play a part in the unusual incidents that have been reported throughout the years.

Visitors to the Excelsior Springs Golf Course Club House have reported doors opening and closing by unseen hands. Others have spied shadowy figures silently traveling between the doorways of the cabin. Small objects are frequently found in unexpected places in the restaurant area connected to the former frontier home.

These events may also be tied to what has become known as the Battle of Fredericksburg. The skirmish began exactly three months after the attack on Jesse O'Dell during the afternoon of July 17, 1864. A Union force of nearly 140 men patrolling the area between the Clay and Ray County lines had split into three smaller groups and set out in search of Rebel bushwhackers thought to be in the area. Forty-seven men from the 2nd Colorado Regiment led by Capt. Thomas Moses had been riding for four days and were searching for food and fresh horses when they happened to spot a group of mounted soldiers in Union blue. They mistakenly assumed the soldiers were friendly forces. Capt. Lymann Rouell was sent ahead to discern the identities of the newcomers. He rode up within 150 feet of the group and waited for a member of the approaching force to come forward to meet him. A few choice and unprintable words were exchanged, and it quickly became apparent that the unidentified riders were a Rebel force in disguise. Shots were fired, and the fighting began.

Eventually it was determined that this group was an advance force of about 70 men led by Capt. Charles Fletcher "Fletch" Taylor, who had previously ridden with William Quantrill's band. The number of total guerrilla forces in the area was nearly 300. Bullets began to fly at the Union forces, and although they were drastically outnumbered, they dismounted and returned fire, ultimately engaging in hand-to-hand combat. Soon the horses became frightened and difficult to manage. To avoid being routed, Captain Moses ordered a retreat, and the Federal forces separated into small groups, abandoning horses, equipment, and six fallen comrades.

The next day, the Union forces returned with 200 reinforcements. On the battlefield, they found the six departed soldiers from their ranks. The bodies had been stripped of all weapons, valuables, and clothing. A merchant from Fredericksburg by the name of Jerry Isley gathered the dead and then used a lumber wagon to transport the fallen Union soldiers to Pisgah Baptist Church. Pisgah Baptist Church was organized in the 1840s by the late Rev. Robert James, the father of Frank and Jesse James. The deceased soldiers were laid out on benches and prepared for burial. They were interred together in a single mass grave. Many of the details of this story were gleaned from articles written by Harry A. Soltysiak, printed in the *Northland Star* newspaper on February 21, 1990, and the *Marketplace* in June 1989. Also contributing to the timeline greatly were events detailed in *Jesse James, The Last Rebel of the Civil War*, by T.J. Stiles.

Sixteen dead from the Rebel forces were discovered on the battlefield. A local businessman and Southern sympathizer, Louis Seybold, allowed locals to bury the guerrillas in his family cemetery behind his tavern, which at one time stood on Seybold Avenue.

Harry A. Soltysiak conducted considerable research at the bequest of the Excelsior Springs Publishing Company into the events that unfolded at the Battle of Fredericksburg during the Civil War at the Excelsior Springs Golf Course. He came to the conclusion that there may have been two skirmishes on the O'Dell property during the summer of 1864, with the second battle taking place on August 12, and that over the course of the past 100 years the two events have become intertwined. This would help to explain why the marker on the 15th tee reads: "In memory of the soldiers of the Civil War who gave their lives at the Battle of Fredericksburg–August 12, 1864."

Two men in the company with Captain Taylor and quite possibly involved in the first skirmish on July 17, 1864, were the soon-to-be-infamous brothers Frank and Jesse James. Frank had joined up with the state guard at the age of 18 in May 1861, just one month following the official declaration of War Between the States. Jesse was a youth of 13 at the time his brother left for battle and would wait until May 1864 before joining into the conflict himself.

During this same period, Frank James had been seasoned in battle. He had been involved in the Battle of Lexington, Missouri, where he became ill and was left behind when the Confederate troops retreated. He surrendered, was paroled, and returned home to the James family farm. By early 1863, Frank was back in action fighting with a guerrilla band under the command of Fernando Scott.

On May 20, 1863, Frank was encamped at Missouri City in Clay County near the banks of the Fishing River. That night, three Union soldiers were killed within their camp. The group then pillaged Missouri City. Within a week of the pillaging, Frank and others were reported to be encamped in the woods somewhere in the vicinity of his family farm when Union militiamen attacked young Jesse and the other members of his family. Additional details of the horrific attack on the James family farm are included in the following section.

Frank's commander, Fernando Scott, was killed during fighting in June near Westport, Missouri, about 40 miles to the south. Frank briefly returned home again but left quickly to begin fighting under the command of William Clark Quantrill. Frank James was probably among the men involved in the massive attack and killing of 200 civilians in Lawrence, Kansas, on August 21, 1863.

After spending a winter in Texas, Frank returned to Clay County in April 1864 with a small squad under the command of Capt. Charles Fletcher Taylor. He was accompanied by Archie Clement, a small but experienced and knowledgeable gunman who would later become close friends with Frank's younger brother, Jesse.

Upon Frank's return, Jesse James, now 16 years old, made the decision to fight alongside his brother and quickly joined up with the group. In the days leading up to the Fredericksburg skirmish, they were involved in wartime events in nearby Missouri cities. On July 6, they were

Fletch Taylor was a close friend and ally of Frank and Jesse James during the Civil War. That friendship continued after the war, although Fletch Taylor escaped the outlaw career of the James Gang and became a successful businessman. (From the Ellison Collection.)

Jesse James's cousin Zee Mimms (center) nursed him through the wounds he received during the Civil War. After his recovery, she was said to have spent most of her time at the home of Zerelda Samuel, which is when this photograph is believed to have been taken. Pictured to the left is Jesse's sister Susan, and on the right is Jesse's half-sister Fannie Quantrill Samuel. (From of the Ellison Collection.)

involved in an attack on Parkville, and on July 10 they were a part of the attack on Platte City. Taylor then ordered his men to return to Clay County. It is not a stretch to assume that Frank and Jesse were in the company of Capt. "Fletch" Taylor on July 17 in Fredericksburg in Clay County, Missouri, and participated in the battle, but it is also possible that by July 17 Frank and Jesse had left this company to catch up with "Bloody" Bill Anderson.

The confusion between the two separate battle dates is understandable, because records place Frank James, Jesse James, and Bill Anderson among the men involved in yet another of many skirmishes taking place along the line between Ray County and Clay County, Missouri, during the summer of 1864, this one on August 12. It is then reported that they moved out of the area to the east on the fateful day of August 13, 1864, when Jesse received a bullet wound to his chest.

Captain Taylor was in all probability only present at the first battle on this property on July 17, 1864, and not in the area on the later date of August 12. To expand on this research, information was gained from *War of the Rebellion: Official Records of the Union and Confederate Armies.* Generally referred to as the *OR Books,* these massive volumes contain reports from officers in the fields that came back to commanding officers at headquarters and the daily order books. Accounts gleaned from these records are as reliable as the person recording them at the time, according to how they needed their daily actions recorded, which means they do have room for human error, human exaggeration, and intentional and unintentional omissions.

As referenced in the *OR* series 1, volume XLI, part 1, serial number 83, page 258, on August 18, 1864, Capt. E.W. Kingsbury of the 2nd Colorado writes to Maj. Nelson Smith of learning that Taylor was headed for Lafayette County, having been severely wounded. Also in series 1, volume XLI, part 41, number 82, serial number 84, page 622, commanding officer J.H. Ford reports that on August 9 in Independence, he had a fight with Fletch Taylor and returned fire. Captain Taylor was seriously wounded.

Shedding some light on the latter event is a description of the skirmish that took place on or near the same location in August 1864 from an article written in the *Excelsior Springs Daily Standard* on September 30, 1936, some 72 years after these events unfolded. The article is based on the memories of "Uncle Dick," otherwise known as Richard Bates. As a young boy, he places the event of a skirmish near Fredericksburg in August 1864. He relates that "a bunch of us had been returning from a church meeting when we ran into a group of the Redlegs [Union soldiers]" prior to a battle at Fredericksburg later the same day and were able to escape from harm after some quick thinking and even quicker riding away.

According to Richard Bates's recollections, around noon, members of his family heard firing from up the road. They did not take young Richard with them but later related witnessing a group of the Redlegs engaged in stripping a widow's home. They reported to him that Jesse James "picked off two Redlegs outposts, and the rest of them scattered from the farmhouse." The two groups then began hand-to-hand combat until the Redlegs retreated to Fredericksburg to make a stand. He also states, "The bodies of the six Redleg casualties were buried in a common grave in the Pisgah church yard."

Richard's retelling of the events mentions the name Thrailkill, which may have been a variation of the name Quantrill brought on by the passage of over seven decades. Current research has not been able to accurately confirm that William Quantrill was in the area at this time.

Another account of the events taking place on August 12, 1864, was printed in the *Richmond News* on October 17, 1987, by John Crouch. The article is helpful in describing Fredericksburg as a small town that was originally named Butter in 1835. Fredericksburg was known for the Essex House stagecoach inn, which served the Butterfield Stage Company. This inn and the town saloon drew soldiers to the area as a familiar resting place. According to this research, five Union men were killed just south of Fredericksburg and buried in a common grave in the Pisgah churchyard.

This stone with a brass marker can be found near the 15th tee of the Excelsior Springs Golf Course. The marker is dedicated to those who lost their lives during the battle of Fredericksburg; a small town once existed in the area. Some key Civil War figures are rumored to have been involved in the fighting on this land, including Frank and Jesse James. (Photograph by Joesph Kline.)

In 1912, the Excelsior Springs Golf Club, pictured here in the 1920s, opened with nine holes. Maj. William A. Bell of Sussex, England, landscape architect George Kessler, and Charles Fish formed the General Realty and Mineral Water and assisted in the creation of the mineral water system on the golf course. (From the private collection of Betty Bissell.)

Golf Hill Drive from Hair Pin Curve,
Excelsior Springs, Mo.—1
"Missouri's National Health Resort"

By 1928, the Excelsior Springs Golf Club boasted a 36-hole course. The O'Dell cabin was enclosed by glass and connected to golf course clubhouse, which offered seating for up to 100 guests for lunch. The golf course drive is pictured here in the 1920s. (From the private collection of Betty Bissell.)

Excelsior Springs: Haunted Haven

The article lists Union soldiers who died in the battle at Fredericksburg as George O'Dell, Phillip Siegel, John Hutchings, Smith Hutchings, and Capt. Patton Colley. Descendents of Phillip Siegel know that his body was not buried in the common grave with his fallen companions.

At some point later in the day, long after the battle, Phillip Siegel's horse returned home alone. The empty saddle was more than enough to inform his family of his sad fate. The family quickly hid the horse in the barn, fearing that bushwhackers might still be in the area. Under the cover of darkness, family members silently crept back to the scene of the bloodshed and spirited his body away.

Phillip was laid to rest in the family cemetery under his enlisted name of Phillip Siel. Aliases were frequently employed by men in the area who chose to serve in the Union army in an attempt to protect their families from local retribution. Phillip and his brother Jacob both enlisted with the alias of Siel, which may have been an anagram of their German mother's maiden name of Icel or simply dropping two letters from their legal name of Siegel.

While the history of the skirmishes on this property are so entangled in the multiple military clashes throughout Clay and Ray Counties during those terrifying days of the Civil War, the story of the creation of the Excelsior Springs Golf Course itself is connected to a later owner of the property, Maj. William A. Bell of Sussex, England. Major Bell helped to form the General Realty and Mineral Water Company in 1910 along with landscape architect George Kessler and Charles Fish. This corporation assisted in the creation of the mineral water system on the golf course. In 1912, the golf club opened with the first nine holes. The cabin was partially enclosed by glass, connecting it to the clubhouse, with seating up to 100 guests for lunch. With several additions by 1928, the Excelsior Springs Golf Club boasted an expansive 36-hole course.

The current English-style clubhouse was constructed around the original O'Dell family cabin in 1969. Although nothing remains of the original loft and a concrete floor has been added to assist in supporting the foundation, the cabin is still in nearly pristine condition and serves as an excellent window into daily life of the past. The O'Dell cabin home is open to the public and is listed in the Clay County Register of Historic Places.

Jesse James Farm and Museum

It is well worth taking the short 15-minute drive to the northwest of Excelsior Springs, just outside of the city of Kearney, Missouri, to discover the Jesse James Farm and Museum. Follow the signs along scenic country roads to the museum, where helpful tour guides will lead the way to the cabin nestled on the hillside in the valley below.

Here at the farmhouse, visitors have the opportunity to stand beside the marker of what was once the grave of Jesse James, just a few steps outside of his rural boyhood home. His remains have since been moved to the family plot in nearby Mount Olivet Cemetery. On the headstone, one can clearly read the engraved dates of "SEPT. 5, 1847 MURDERED APR. 3, 1882." The 34 short years spanning the life of Jesse James were some of the most turbulent and violent times this nation has ever seen. It is hard to imagine the tragic events that took place on this land while one stands on this peaceful spot on a quiet grassy hillside.

The farmhouse where Jesse James was born is a simple and unassuming cabin built in 1822, making it one of the earliest structures in Clay County, Missouri. The James family arrived to work the 275-acre farm in October 1845, more than 35 years before the healing waters in Excelsior Springs were discovered. The family at that time consisted of the Reverend Robert James, his wife Zerelda Cole James, and their young son, Alexander Franklin James. Their son Jesse Woodson James was born in the cabin on September 5, 1847.

One of the earliest structures in Clay County, Missouri, the Jesse James family farm was built in 1822. The small cabin became home to the Reverend Robert James, his wife Zerelda Cole James, and their young son Alexander Franklin James in 1845. In the cabin on September 5, 1847, Zerelda gave birth to her second son, Jesse Woodson James. (Author's collection.)

As young men, Jesse (left) and Frank James were considered upper class, as their father was a Baptist preacher credited with starting several churches and William Jewel College. After his death in 1850, their lives were troubled, as their mother struggled to hang on to that lifestyle. This image was taken sometime after Zerelda married Dr. Reuben Samuel. (From the Ellison Collection.)

It takes just a few steps and a short tour through the nearby James Farm Museum to fully comprehend the episodes and their aftermath, which spun the sadness, terror, and strength of this small farming family into a legend and a legacy that will remain a vital part of the fabric of American history. Here at the museum perhaps are the clues to the causes of the paranormal activity reported both at the farm and at the museum itself.

Fortunately, museum tour guide Linda helped lead me in the right direction, for she had shared with me in advance a few reports of ghostly events at this historic location. The PEDRO team accompanied me that day on a quest to the Jesse James Farm and Museum to tie the stories with actual events from the past. Joining us was one of our newest team members, Fred, along with Joe and Mitzi, both seasoned paranormal researchers.

It had been originally been my conjecture, based on the events as Linda described them, that the paranormal activity taking place at this location might be a result of a "residual energy" haunting, since events very similar in nature were reported over a period of time. Troy Taylor, founder of the American Ghost Society, provides the following explanation for residual energy:

> Many of these locations, where these hauntings take place, experience an event or a series of events, which imprints itself on the atmosphere of a place. This event can suddenly discharge and play itself at various times. The events are not always visual either; they are often replayed as sounds and noises that have no explanation. Often the sounds and images recorded are related to traumatic events that took place at the location and caused some sort of disturbance, which we might call "psychic impression," to happen there.

Here is the tale as it was personally related to tour guide Linda. At one point in time, a caretaker was assigned to live in an apartment beneath the museum to keep watch on the property both day and night. On several occasions, he was awakened in the middle of the night to the sounds of shouting voices and of horses near the cabin. On each occasion, he was certain that intruders were on the museum grounds. He would quickly dress and rush to the location of the ruckus. And every time, upon reaching the cabin, the sounds would fade away. Doing his duty, he carefully searched the grounds on these late-night excursions, but he was unable to locate trespassers or even any visible signs that the ground around the cabin had been disturbed.

With the assistance of historic interpreters, powerfully moving museum exhibits, and research found in *The James Farm, Its People, Their Lives, Their Times* by Martin McGrane, two events were found to be intense enough in nature to be likely candidates for creating the "psychic impression" witnessed by the caretaker over the years.

The first tragic event occurred during the summer of 1863. By this time, Zerelda was married to her third husband, Dr. Reuben Samuel. Frank James was away fighting, and Jesse was nearing his 16th birthday. It would be many years before Jesse penned an account of that fateful day.

Jesse was some distance from the cabin working in the cornfield when he watched soldiers arrive searching for his brother, Frank. The soldiers attempted to force Zerelda to tell them where her eldest son could be found. Zerelda explained he was not on the property and she did not know where he could be found. She also denied all accusations that she and her son Jesse were supplying Quantrill with supplies and information.

The soldiers became more aggressive and did their best to gain money and information from Dr. Samuel. Unsuccessful, they dragged him to a nearby tree and used a "dry hanging" method in an attempt to force information out of him. Dry hanging consists of hanging a person nearly to the point of death and then releasing the rope in an attempt to bring them into submission. When these brutal efforts failed, they hung him one last time and left him alone in the woods to slowly strangle to death.

Zerelda James Samuel was known as a tough character. She outlived three husbands and is seen here shortly before a bomb thrown into her home by the Pinkerton Detective Agency took off the lower portion of her right arm and killed her young son Archie. The agency had hoped to capture Jesse and Frank James. (From the Ellison Collection.)

The second stepfather of Frank and Jesse James was a quiet but prominent man until his beating by Union troops during the Civil War. After that event, Dr. Samuel would never regain his prominence, but he was very loved by the three James children, Frank, Jesse, and Susan. He and Zerelda had several children of their own. (From the Ellison Collection.)

Well dressed and manicured, Jesse James appears to be a fine, upstanding citizen. His clean-cut look indicates his religious upbringing. His fierce expression reflects the pain of seeing his stepfather tortured by Union troops. The image was probably taken right before going to war, which changed the direction of his life forever. (From the Ellison Collection.)

The men again turned their attentions to Zerelda, who was clearly very pregnant at the time. One soldier shoved her across the room, slamming her into the wall and nearly ripping her dress off in the process. Next, the men overtook Jesse working at his plow in the cornfields. The soldiers began beating Jesse with bayonets and whipping him with the plow lines. Zerelda begged for her son's life, but the men continued their violence against him.

When the militia finally tired of beating young Jesse, they took their leave. Zerelda then rushed into the woods to cut down her husband, Dr. Samuel. The poor man was barely alive, and it took time and patience for Zerelda to nurse him back to health. Sadly, due to oxygen depravation from the repeated hangings, Dr. Samuel was disabled for the rest of his days.

The second unfortunate event at the country cabin occurred in 1875. Between these years, so many events filled the lives of the James-Samuel family that they could and have filled many volumes of literature. During the intervening years, Jesse joined his brother Frank in the war, the war came to an end, and they began their careers as the most well-publicized bank robbers in America. This author will leave those events to others far more educated in the multitude of events surrounding the war and its aftermath and will jump forward in time to January 1875.

It was a cold, wintery night, and men hired by the Pinkerton Agency of Chicago advanced on the cabin. They had arrived in hopes of arresting Frank and Jesse James on information provided by undercover agent Jack Ladd. Ladd had been able to pass himself off as a farmhand on the neighboring farm of Daniel Askew. From this nearby vantage point, he thought he had witnessed the return of the famous pair of brothers and reported it immediately.

The men who gathered around the cabin that night were under orders to use whatever force necessary to apprehend the fugitives. They shattered a window, terrifying the inhabitants inside. Before any of the family had a chance to protect themselves, a flaming wad of cotton batting that had been soaked in turpentine flew through the open space. Dr. Samuel later related that the family used tobacco sticks to pick the fiery mass up off the floor and throw it into the fireplace, thus putting themselves out of harm's way.

Since this tactic worked well the first time, Dr. Samuel took similar fast action with a shovel when a second object flew in from the shattered window. Unfortunately this object of destruction was a heavy iron ball filled with a flammable liquid that caused a horrible explosion when it was launched by the shovel into the fireplace. Dr. Samuel was thrown so hard he hit the ceiling. Zerelda's right arm was so severely damaged it had to be amputated, leaving her forever maimed from the incident. Saddest of all, while the men were shouting a victory cheer outside, the family discovered their young son Archie Payton Samuel had been killed in the blast. Jesse and Frank James were nowhere in sight and perhaps had not even been in the cabin on this tragic evening.

PEDRO has yet to investigate these grounds at night to further explore the reported paranormal disturbances. Could it be that one or both horrible incidents are replaying themselves over and over again near the anniversaries of these life-altering events?

The investigative team was drawn to explore possibilities of other spirit activities at the museum building as well. The entire PEDRO team was astounded at the artifacts inside the museum. It was a great delight to stand within inches of a shotgun, cartridge belt, handkerchief, and other items owned by Jesse James. Even saddles used by Jesse, Frank, and Frank's wife Annie, were on display.

Several other items were spotted by the team that could have possible links to paranormal activity. Among them was the original headstone of Archie Samuel and the embalming table used upon the death of Jesse James. On the embalming table rests the original lid to Jesse James casket. The casket was replaced due to deterioration when his remains were transported to the family plot.

Allan Pinkerton and his son Robert were instrumental in developing the public image of Jesse James and the James Gang. Due to the Pinkertons' mishaps while trying to capture them, public opinion turned in favor of the James boys. (From of the Ellison Collection.)

Frank James is thought by some to be the true leader of the James Gang. As Jesse James's older brother, he was well read and often quoted Shakespeare. Here he is seen in the prime of their outlaw years in the early 1870s. (From the Ellison Collection.)

Frank James became a much sought-after commodity after he was acquitted of all crimes of which he had been accused. A Wild West Show and horse-race starter were just a few of his public jobs. This photograph appears to have been taken after he was a free man. (From the Ellison Collection.)

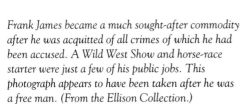

Donnie Pence served in the war with Jesse and Frank James and was said to have been in on at least one robbery with the gang. He later went straight and became a law officer, as did many of the ex-Confederates. (From of the Ellison Collection.)

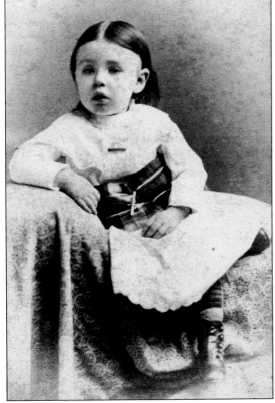

The daughter of Jesse James is seen here at about three years of age wearing a black mourning sash, which was proper at that time after a death. Mary had no memory of her father, and her mother never revealed any of his activities to her. (From of the Ellison Collection.)

After our trip to the museum, I again contacted our guide Linda and asked if there had been any activity reported in the museum. I explained further that although the museum was built many years later, in 1986 spirits attaching themselves to personal objects is something we have come across frequently. Linda responded that there were reports of paranormal activity in the museum building, although these particular occurrences were extremely rare.

Reported in separate incidents, two different women described feeling movement or a distinctive physical tug on their bra straps—which was something unusual to report. With the large amount of personal objects in the museum from a wide variety of donors, it may be difficult to pin down the exact object or the lecherous phantom tied to these remarkable events. Hopefully, more guests will experience something similar and report future otherworldly touches, which might help to narrow down the possibilities.

The James Farm
21216 James Farm Road
Kearney, MO 64060
Phone: (816) 736-8500
Hours (May–September):
Monday–Sunday, 9:00 a.m.–4:00 p.m.
Hours (October–April):
Monday–Saturday, 9:00 a.m.–4:00 p.m.
Sunday, 12:00 p.m.–4:00 p.m.
Admission:
Adults—$7.50
Seniors (62 and over)—$6.50
Children (8–15)—$4
Children (Under 8)—Free
Discounts available for groups of 15 or more.
www.jessejames.org

ODD FELLOWS HOME AND BELVOIR WINERY

A quick 20-minute drive to the southwest of Excelsior Springs is all it takes to discover the grandeur of the former Independent Order of Odd Fellows (IOOF) Home in Liberty, Missouri, with 170 acres, six historic buildings, and a tucked-away cemetery. The majority of the buildings on this historic property are listed in the National Register of Historic Places.

The long, picturesque stairway leading down the hillside from the current home of the Belvoir Winery is just the first of many amazingly delightful architectural details that will catch and please the visitor's eye. Many brides slowly descend these steps to the ornate white gazebo at the base of the hill to take their wedding vows. Or they can choose a storybook entrance in a white carriage with red velvet seating pulled by Jessica and Beauty, two statuesque Clydesdale horses who live in the stables at the crest of the hill.

In 1887, three mineral water springs were discovered on this property that were reported to possess healing properties similar to the springs gaining popularity in nearby Excelsior Springs and other similar sites across the nation. The grand Winner Hotel was quickly constructed with over 100 guest rooms. Over-the-top amenities for hotel guests consisted of a pari-mutuel horse track, a lake complete with boats and a boathouse, a bowling alley, and a 2,500-person outdoor pavilion. The hotel was later sold and renamed the Reed Springs Hotel. The first two owners

Pictured here striking a similar pose are believed to be, from left to right, Billy the Kid, Doc Holliday, Jesse James, and Charlie Bowdre. Doc wears a six-star badge, while the others present white flags to show they are deputized. A ghostly female figure stands to the right of Charlie, and he happened to be the only one of the four who was married at the time. All four men were known to have been in Las Vegas, New Mexico, in July 1879. Of note, the majority of these photographs of Jesse James, his family, and his gang have never appeared in a publication before this time. It is also the first publication to present the Jesse James portion of the Ellison Collection as a whole. (From the Ellison Collection.)

The current home of the luxurious Belvoir Winery began as the Independent Order of the Odd Fellows Orphanage, which was constructed in 1900 as a part of the mission of the organization. (Author's collection.)

This photograph of Mary Elizabeth Saltar taken while her family was visiting for her birthday on February 14, 1934, near the front steps of the old folk's home. Mary passed away later in the year, due in part to a massive heat wave. (From the private collection of the Belvoir Winery.)

This is a photograph of Gene Campbell taken while he was visiting his grandmother Mary Elizabeth Saltar on her birthday, February 14, 1934. Much of the old folk's home can be seen in the background. (From the private collection of the Belvoir Winery.)

General View of the Odd Fellows Home, Liberty Mo.

This postcard depicts the front of the old folk's home portion of the Odd Fellows complex. The back of the postcard is dated 1910. This is the building where Mary Elizabeth Saltar and others lived during the great heat wave of 1934. (From of the private collection of the Belvoir Winery.)

lasted only a dozen years between them. The property was purchased by the Independent Order of Odd Fellows in early 1899.

Very early in 1900, the hotel felt the icy chill of a normal harsh Midwestern winter, and the hotel staff discovered early one morning that many of the pipes in the building had frozen solid overnight. Someone thought it would be a good idea to try to use blowtorches to quickly warm the pipes and get the water flowing once again. Instead, sparks from the torches set the building on fire. The entire structure burned to the ground.

The replacement building, which was planned for use as an orphanage, was constructed in 1900. This new building was designed to be as fireproof as possible for the time. Most of the structure of the building is brick, steel, and concrete, saving the aesthetic wooden touches for last. The floors are a solid nine and a half inches of concrete topped with nine inches of burned coal. The burned coal was an ingenious concept, adding both insulation and an additional layer of fire retardant to the structure. The orphanage building is over 50,000 square feet in size and served as a home and a school for disadvantaged children for many years. The Odd Fellows Orphanage was advanced for its time, possessing running water and electric lights long before much of the nearby city of Liberty.

During the Depression era, the orphanage became more like a communal home or county poor farm. Possessing nearly 300 acres of land, the home became virtually self-sufficient by raising livestock, growing produce, and trading the excess for any additional needs. As additional structures were added to the complex, the orphanage became known as the administration building.

Between the mid-1950s and the early 1970s, the administration building was utilized as a school for the growing Liberty School District. The district revitalized an area on the third floor that had served as classrooms for the children during the building's many years as an orphanage. Blackboards and coat hooks can still be seen in these classrooms by visitors today. Here on the third floor, small, soft footsteps have been heard by guests below, and the playful giggling of little children has echoed softy down the stairwells.

Continuing the mission of the Odd Fellows, in 1906 an old folk's home was built on the property. Much larger in size, the old folk's home is between 80,000 and 90,000 square feet. The building has a very institutional feel, with long, narrow hallways and small resident rooms. There are also a few small meeting rooms, a kitchen, and a lobby area. The new owners have noticed that among the many resident rooms, a few have padlocks on the outside of the doors for securing the occupant safely inside.

The old hospital on the Odd Fellows grounds was constructed in 1920. For over 30 years, this was the only hospital in Clay County, Missouri. Its usefulness began to end with the advent of modern hospital gurneys. The new gurneys were too wide for two to be used in the same hallway at the same time. This resulted in serious delays as one gurney was backed up or stood waiting in a nearby hallway for another to pass.

The most recent structure, the "modern" nursing home, was added to the complex next door to the administration building in 1955. This final structure has two stories and contains roughly 30 rooms for patients. It is of brick construction with a flat roof. It was attached to the old folk's home directly to the west by a single hallway. The nursing home continued over the years as a small operation and finally closed its doors in the mid-1980s. It has been estimated that between the old folk's home and the hospital somewhere between 7,000 and 10,000 people have died on the property.

One remarkable story that may or may not be linked to the current stories of ghostly activity on the property is based on the difficulties faced by the elderly residents of the IOOF Old Folk's Home during the record heat wave of 1934. It was at the height of the Great Depression, and times were tough throughout the country. Adding to the difficulties of rising unemployment

This postcard from the 1950s depicts the front of the administration building, which formerly housed the Odd Fellows Orphanage. (From of the private collection of the Belvoir Winery.)

This paper airplane folded from the pages of a magazine stayed nestled inside a classroom wall on the third floor for over 90 years. (From of the private collection of the Belvoir Winery.)

Several small objects found during renovations at the Belvoir Winery depict the lives of the children who lived on the property at the Odd Fellows Orphanage. Perhaps these objects found on the third floor, where the children went to school, are linked to the paranormal experiences emanating from this area of the building. (From of the private collection of the Belvoir Winery.)

was a series of droughts and massive heat waves that caused extensive damage to crops in the Midwest and turned the fertile cropland in the heart of America into the Dust Bowl.

Mary Elizabeth Saltar wrote home to her family, reporting, "It has sure been hot here. I have felt it very much. Everything is burning up here too, and it seems to be everywhere. We will have no vegetables to speak of this winter; the hot, dry weather has burned the gardens up. This weather has been very hard on old people. We have had six deaths within a month." Sadly, before the summer was through, Mary Saltar passed away as well. Her family has kindly given permission to tell her story. To date, research has uncovered at least eight additional deaths at the old folk's home between June and August 1934, with the majority of the deceased being laid to rest in the cemetery on the hill.

The complex contains four original outbuildings as well. The coal-burning power plant still stands behind the orphanage but was severely damaged many years ago in a fire. Two small garages have held their own against the ravages of time. An underground bunker has served several purposes over the past century, including cold food storage, a storm shelter, and during the atomic era of the 1950s and early 1960s as a bomb shelter.

Behind all of these buildings, barely visible on the hillside above, is a small cemetery containing about 600 nearly identically marked graves. The vast majority of the residents who passed away on the property were claimed by their loved ones and are buried in other locations. The 600 interred at the hillside cemetery represent several groups, including children with no family from the orphanage, the elderly with no one to claim them, and a few members of the Odd Fellows or its sister organization the Rebecca Lodge who chose to make the cemetery their final resting place. The oldest date that has been located on the headstones is a birth date in 1830.

It is uncertain if the cemetery is home to any paranormal activity, but it is known that the cemetery was originally directly beside the orphanage. The headstones, along with the bodies interred, were moved to the hillside location some time near 1910. The move was required due to two factors: the first was the rapid expansion and use of the complex portion of the grounds; the second reason was that the number of graves in the cemetery grew beyond the original platted area needed to contain them. A journey up the hill to the cemetery will also reveal a World War II memorial dedicated to six members of the Odd Fellows lodge who gave their lives in the line of duty. The cemetery is right next to the vineyards. Some jokingly remark that this is perhaps the reason why the wine from the Belvoir Winery tastes so good.

Whether one is curious about history, ghosts, or just wants to sample wines from a unique and hauntingly beautiful Missouri winery, a trip to Belvoir Winery is worth the time. The new owners have done more than just restore the former orphanage into a workable building; they have gone above and beyond, gathering unique antique pieces to display to their guests. Stop by for a wine tasting and listen closely for the sound of soft footsteps and gentle laughter emanating from the floors above.

Jesse Leimkuehler, the current manager of the Belvoir Winery, related his own ghost experience on the property. It happened around 7:00 a.m. on what would later turn out to be a very hot day in August 2010. Jesse had arrived early but was expecting one other worker to be poking around somewhere within the administration building. He entered through the front entrance, which at that stage of the renovations was the only workable access to the building.

He clearly heard another person walking around on the second floor. The clear, loud, heavy thump of a man walking about was unmistakable. So thinking he would join in on the work on the second floor, Jesse headed up the stairs. Each floor is sizable, and it took Jesse some time treading down the separate hallways looking for his companion on the second floor to come to the realization that he was indeed alone in the building.

Still looking about on the second floor, Jesse spied the other worker out of a back window. The other man was working outside near the barn on the hillside more than a fifth of a mile

Just 15 miles east of Excelsior Springs in Richmond, Missouri, is the 100-year-old Ray County Historical Society Museum. This 54-room, Georgian-style former institution sits on top of a small bluff dominating the scenery around it. (Author's collection.)

away. Since the front door at that time was the only way in and out of the property, Jesse knew the other man could not have passed by him without being seen, let alone have travelled such a great distance in such a short period of time. Jesse described his overall impression of the experience briefly, "It wasn't frightening at all. What it didn't do was make me want to run from the building. But, the experience left me with the realization that I am never entirely alone in the building."

Belvoir Winery
1325 Odd Fellows Road
Liberty, MO 64068
For reservations, e-mail info@belvoirwinery.com
Phone: (816) 200-1811
www.belvoirwinery.com
Open year-round, excluding holidays
10:00 a.m.–8:00 p.m.
12:00 p.m.–6:00 p.m. Sundays
"Your perfect spot for weddings, receptions, birthday parties, and private events."

RAY COUNTY HISTORICAL SOCIETY MUSEUM

In nearby Richmond, Missouri, 15 miles east of Excelsior Springs, is the home of the Ray County Historical Society Museum. This massive redbrick historical site sits on top of a small bluff facing the town square and dominates the scenery around it. Construction of the 54-room, Georgian-style former institution began in September 1908. By May 1910, the Ray County Poor Farm opened its doors to approximately 50 residents. These residents were moved from the former, older, and much smaller establishment 11 miles to the north. At the time, this brand-new structure with electricity and steam heating was possibly the most modern building in Ray County, Missouri. There have been some scattered reports that the building of the new home and the quick move of the residents was due to condemning reports from the state of the horrific state of affairs at the previous county home.

The extensive complex with 23 acres of land was large enough for growing a wide variety of garden crops. There was also room allotted for raising cattle, hogs, workhorses, and chickens. Additional land was available for a slaughterhouse, a smokehouse, and a small pond out front for fishing and swimming. The facility with the surrounding grounds was nearly self-sufficient, with many of the live-in residents assisting in the day-to-day operations and production of produce. Nearly every able-bodied resident found a task or quickly learned a skill that aided in the functioning of the home. When necessary, goods produced on this farm complex were traded or sold in nearby towns in exchange for required supplies. Receipts have been located and placed in the archives at the museum documenting purchases for items such as salt, flour, beds, and mattresses, among other basic needs.

A barn on the property once housed a wagon and the workhorses that were used to haul grain back from town. The horse-drawn wagon took a long winding path around the east side of the building to a loading shoot that sent supplies directly down into the basement.

A small shed behind the building has been discovered to be the remains of the smokehouse. The building now holds several sets of rusting prison bars moved at some point in the past from the site of the original Ray County Poor Farm. These rusting bars are all that remain of a location that was at one time called "unfit even for the vermin that inhabited it." This building has also acquired a small family of raccoons often seen playing about in the area directly behind the kitchen steps.

Over the course of time, as occupants passed away, two cemeteries were added on the grounds. To the north is the City Cemetery. This graveyard is now barely discernible, as many of the headstones have eroded and broken over time and still more grave sites have been moved to family plots in other locations. A smaller cemetery containing a potter's field is on the southern edge of the property with roughly 40 burials and only one small original headstone. A larger marker, placed as an Eagle Scout project in 2001, bears a list of some of the residents known to be interred on this small plot of ground.

The Ray County Poor Farm, which was normally filled to capacity with approximately 50 residents, continued day-to-day operations until 1959. The next incarnation of the dwelling began later that same year, when it reopened as the Elms Park Rest Home. In this commercial, for-profit institution, management received payment per head for the number of people housed in the facility. The situation changed for the worse with a drastic increase in the number of beds in each room. In some cases, four to five beds were squeezed into each room with barely enough room for guests to stand or walk between them. The status quo of overcrowding continued up until 1971.

As Karen Bush, executive director of the Ray County Museum, sat in her office near the front of the massive former county poor farm building, she explained that the current museum business office was once the formal sitting parlor. She often feels as if the former caretakers of this expansive location watch over her while she works, especially while she is cleaning, stating:

When I'm sweeping the grand staircase I become aware of someone watching over my shoulder making certain I don't miss any dust. You can almost picture in your mind someone pointing out a missed speck here or there. I have often gotten the sensation of their approval on the care of their building.

A story of the grand staircase ties into a former political hopeful who was running for office several years ago. This overly confident politician decided that the best campaign publicity stills could be shot on the grand staircase at the Ray County Museum. Doing what comes naturally to any would-be elected official, he went about setting up the photo shoot with as much pomp and circumstance and disruption to the daily routine of the museum as possible.

It quickly became apparent that using the main staircase as a backdrop for the photographs was not a good idea. The dark oak of the staircase and the dim lighting from the windows made the main subject of the pictures pale in comparison. A second location was chosen, downstairs in the museum office. While the pictures came out better than those on the staircase, each and every photograph had up to three large orbs, which made them useless for the purpose of publicity. Karen Bush was quoted that day saying, "Even though most orbs can easily be explained away, it might be that the residents of the museum are showing their disapproval for the candidate. Perhaps in this case these particular orbs might be a sign this man will not win the race." And, in fact, he did lose in his run for election.

One great ghost story that centered on the location of the grand staircase was many years in the making. Karen visited the site of what is now the Ray County Museum with her daughter, who was a small child at the time. The City of Richmond was fighting to save the historic site by holding a public event at the nearly empty location. For just the briefest fleeting moment, Karen thought she saw what she can only describe as a little man upon the stairs. He was there one moment and then gone in the blink of an eye. Later that evening, Karen mentioned the odd chance meeting on the staircase to her husband. The discussion took place in private, because she did not wish to frighten her young children. Quickly brushing off the incident, Karen thought little about the matter until just a few years ago. She was telling her daughter, who was now an adult, that she had just accepted the position as executive director of the museum. Her daughter answered, "Say hi to the little man for me."

Karen inquired, "What little man?" Her daughter just smiled and said, "You know, the little man on the stairs." Both women had seen the apparition all those many years ago, and neither one had ever mentioned the incident to the other. Karen went on to explain, "It's amazing, if I hadn't gotten this job at the museum, we might never have discovered we shared in a paranormal experience." It is something she has experience with, explaining to visitors that she grew up in a haunted home:

At least that's what we told everyone. There was never any dark shadows lurking about, but whenever anything odd occurred, it was the family custom to blame it on "Georgie" the ghost. That's why when it became evident that the Ray County Museum was haunted, it was only natural to begin calling the ghost George. From then on the name just kind of stuck.

There is the real possibility that one of the ghosts haunting the building could be the spirit of Goldie Riser, who lived practically her entire life in the county poor farm; her life story is heartbreaking. The world first learned of Goldie's tragic tale on October 29, 1896, when the *Richmond Conservator* newspaper covered in very graphic detail the gruesome murder of her mother, three-year-old sister, and 18-month-old baby brother. She was by all accounts deaf and mute her entire life and therefore unable to assist authorities with information about what she may have witnessed during the murder of her entire family.

Little is known of Goldie's life before arriving in the area with her mother, Eva, and stepfather, Jessie, after leaving their former home in Hicksville, Ohio. With no friends, relatives, or business acquaintances in the area, there is was no apparent reason for her parents' choice of moving into the small one-room log cabin in northern Missouri four years earlier. Goldie's mother left her first husband, Goldie's father, and married Jessie Winner on October 28, 1892, in Pauling, Ohio. During their time in the small cabin outside of town, Goldie's mother had given birth to two more children, Goldie's half-sister and half-brother by her mother's second marriage. It has been rumored that Goldie's mother may have been expecting again at the time of her death, but no records have been uncovered to document these speculations.

It was early on an October Tuesday morning when a nearby neighbor by the name of Mr. M.D. Street was headed down the road past the Winner farm and spotted six-year-old Goldie out in the yard acting very strangely. (Newspaper reports on the age of Goldie Riser at this time vary widely from 6 to 12, but research has helped to narrow down the timeline to reveal that she was actually 6 years old at the night her family was killed.) Mr. Street quickly noticed a group of hogs surrounding and feasting on something in the yard just beyond the fence—it was the body of Goldie's mother, still in her nightclothes. After driving the hogs away, Mr. Street alerted the neighbors. Together, they entered the small cabin and discovered the dead body of a three-year-old girl with a slit throat lying on the bed. On the floor at the foot of the bed were the remains of the 18-month-old boy, his throat slashed in a fashion similar to his sister.

Police arrived and searched in vain for clues as to who had committed these murders and any possible motive as to why. Robbery was quickly ruled out, because the small, humble cabin contained only a bed, a cook stove, and two or three chairs and appeared not to have contained anything of value. A subsequent search for evidence pointing to the identity of the assailants was in vain. Goldie was brought into town in an attempt to learn if she had witnessed the murders and could give any information to help in the arrest of the guilty party (or parties). Unschooled and most likely frightened out of her wits, Goldie could only shake her hands about and was unable to properly communicate with those around her.

This photograph was taken in 1896 as a six-year-old Goldie Riser sat at the local police station after the gruesome murder of her mother and two younger siblings. Goldie was an unschooled deaf-mute and could only motion her hands about in a futile attempt to relate her story. (From the Ray County Historical Society and Museum collection.)

It was in this small, rural log cabin where a horrendous triple murder took place. On an early October morning, a woman was found dead in her yard. Inside, her two small children, an 18-month-old boy and a three-year-old girl, were found with their throats cut. An 1890s postcard of Goldie's childhood home was mass-produced after news of the murder of her mother, brother, and sister spread. Justification for the sale of this and other postcards covering the murder was that it was necessary to recoup funds for the cost of Goldie's room and board. (From the Ray County Historical Society and Museum collection.)

Several first-time visitors to the museum have stopped by this room on the second floor in the east wing of the museum. Without any background knowledge of Goldie, guests have commented on feeling the presence of a handicapped woman who is attempting to communicate with them. (Author's collection.)

Another 1890s postcard sold after the triple homicide captured a collection of items suspected to be among the weapons used to brutally murder Goldie's mother. It has been suggested that her mother, Eva Winner, put up quite a struggle. During this struggle, the murderer hit Eva with a chair and then chased her into the yard and hit her with a rail (large piece of wood) and an axe, leaving her body to the elements. (From the Ray County Historical Society and Museum collection.)

Jessie Winner was a coal miner who often spent several days at a time away from his family working in nearby towns when mining work was available. He spent his remaining time at home, raising corn on his farm. He had been away from his small family for several days and was planning on returning soon to gather in his corn crop when he received the horrible news that his entire family except his stepdaughter Goldie had been brutally murdered. Later that same day, Winner was placed into legal custody until the matter could be further investigated.

A formal investigation began by interviewing neighbors near the scene of the triple murder. Mrs. Hankins lived half a mile away in the original county poor farm. She was the wife of the superintendent. She stated she heard three screams late in the night but thought the ruckus was caused by one of the inmates of the poor farm, so she did not pay much attention to the noise. Upon further thought, she felt the screams must have been those of Eva Winner. Neighbors closer to the Winner cabin, such as the Street family only 500 yards away, report they did not hear any sounds in the area. Another neighbor a quarter of a mile away stated that she also did not hear any unusual sounds in the night.

Evidence discovered at the cabin where the murders took place clearly pointed to a long struggle between Eva Winner and her attacker. Blood was spattered in several places on the floor, possibly beginning around the cook stove. Also found were several pieces of a broken chair that was assumed to be the original weapon of the attack. Outside, about eight feet from the cabin near the body of Eva, was a rail (large piece of wood) containing hair strands and still more bloodstains. The final piece of evidence was an axe. After all other attempts had failed, it was clear the assailant took the life of Eva with a strong blow to the top of her head with the axe and left her lifeless body lying in the hog lot.

Within a few days, police arrested Lon Lackey, a close associate of Jessie Winner. As reported later in the *Richmond Conservator*, a preliminary hearing for Jessie Winner and Lon Lackey was held on Monday, November 9, at 10:00 a.m. Both men were charged with the murders of the Winner family of October 16. Attorneys for the defense of both men asked that the matter go before a grand jury. Both cases continued, and the two men were returned to the local jail.

Large crowds had gathered outside in hopes of attending the trial of the two men and to hear the morbid details of the triple murders. By early afternoon, it was clear to everyone a trial would not take place that day, and the crowd quickly turned into an angry mob. The local paper reported, "Harsh words were exchanged." In an attempt to keep the peace, Sheriff Holman deputized 15 to 20 men. After a few more threats were exchanged between the heated rabble and authorities, the crowd slowly dispersed. Back in the jailhouse, rumors quickly arrived that the group planned to return with renewed force before the night was over.

The rumors proved to be true when later that evening over 100 men gathered outside the jail intent on lynching Jesse Winner and Lon Lackey for the murders of the three Winner family members. It was Friday night, about 2:00 a.m., when the sheriff discovered the group outside. The assembly demanded keys to the cell, but the sheriff stated that he had sent the keys home with Deputy Sheriff Green. This sent the crowd on a fool's errand to the deputy's home. When they arrived, the group was informed that the deputy had left town. Returning to the jailhouse with a little less steam than before, they talked for a bit and then gradually left the area.

With the two men's lives in grave jeopardy, the accused were moved secretly to the Lafayette County Jail, across the river in nearby Lexington. On December 10, 1896, the *Richmond Conservator* headline read, "Winner and Nelson Lynched." The angry throng had returned later that night with more vigor than before and this time succeeded in breaking the lock off the cell door and removing the two inmates. The alleged murderers were taken back across the river in a

A picture was taken in 1896 and turned into a postcard of the hanged bodies of Jessie Winner and Lon Lackey. The two men were rumored to be involved in the murders of Goldie Riser's mother and siblings. Winner was living with Goldie's mother, Eva, at the time and was also the father of the two murdered children but was not the father of Goldie. (From the Ray County Historical Society and Museum collection.)

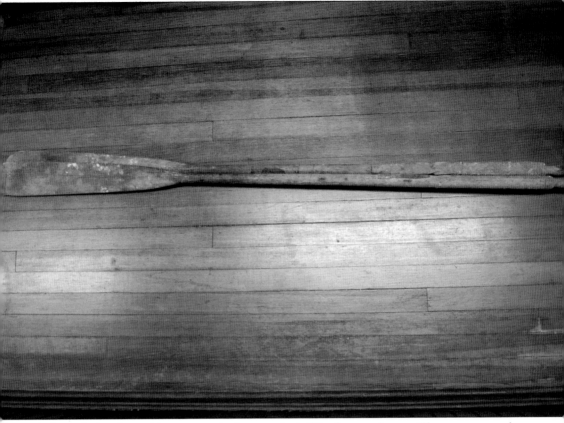

On display at the Ray County Museum is a pair of seven-and-a-half-foot-long wooden oars. These oars were used to row Jessie Winner and Lon Lackey across the river to their fate after a mob broke them out of the Liberty Jail seeking revenge. (Author's collection.)

rowboat to what was then known as Jacks Ferry. The following day, their bodies were discovered by locals hanging together from a burr oak tree.

The ropes used were evidently taken from halters, one of them spliced with a smaller rope. Pieces of the tree upon which the men were hanged were broken off and taken away as mementoes, while the pieces of rope commanded a premium.

The article also states that found in the pockets of Jessie Winner at the time of his death were a brass watch and chain, a funeral card, a piece of tobacco, a handkerchief, a pocketbook containing 15¢, smoking tobacco, a letter, and a memorandum book.

In an odd twist of fate, Jessie Winner's body was later buried in the graveyard at the former county poor farm. His remains were placed near the final resting places of his late wife and his two murdered children. The seven-and-a-half-foot-long oak oars used that cold dark night to row Jesse Winner and Lon Lackey across the river to meet their accusers and end their lives are on display at the Ray County Historical Society Museum.

Goldie's story for the next few years of her life is sketchy at best. Local papers report that during the hearings of Jessie Winner and Lon Lackey, her mother's brother arrived in town to speak with police, but he did not leave with the child. Local residents have given an account that Goldie was temporarily taken in by a kind elderly couple who adored her. Taking her lack of education into account, they sent her for a year to Fulton School for the Deaf. It is not known why Goldie returned just one year later and was placed in the county poor farm only half a mile from the farm where she had witnessed the brutal murder of her family.

Additional research regarding Goldie Riser was uncovered by Cindy Worrall, who feels that in a way Goldie has reached out from across the years and touched her heart. In the 1900 census, six years after the murders, Goldie is listed in two separate places: first, living with Luther and Nannie Snyder, who were 27 and 30 years old; Goldie is also listed as a pupil at the Fulton, Missouri, School for the Deaf, along with many others, including a few adults. It may be that the census records for the two locations were taken at separate times of the year.

Several postcards were mass-produced in the wake of the publicity of theses murders. One postcard was of the small cabin that was Goldie's childhood home. Another postcard clearly featured her murdered mother and siblings displayed out on tables with onlookers gazing upon their stiffening corpses. Upon close examination of this particularly macabre postcard, it appears that Goldie is captured in the photograph standing alone and also gazing on the remains of her mother and siblings. Another grisly postcard was a picture of the two men, Jessie Winner and Lon Lackey, lynched at the side of the river and still dangling from their ropes. These shocking postcards were sold to the public, and the proceeds were received by the poor farm. The justification for the sale and profit from these horrendous keepsakes was to recoup funds for the cost of Goldie's room and board.

What little is known of Goldie's life from that point on is that she must have been among the first residents to move into the grand new location in May 1910. The 1920 census lists Goldie as a Ray County Poor Farm resident. This same census states that she was unable to read or write, but this was not uncommon for the time or the place. Many of the other residents of the home are also listed as unable to read or write.

Goldie did successfully function for the rest of her life as a part of the small community in the Ray County Poor Farm. Local residents still recall seeing her working on several occasions in the kitchen, and she was also seen wandering about on the grounds. Goldie Riser's obituary in 1941 simply states that she passed away at the home at age 51 with no living relatives. Her age was reported incorrectly, for Goldie Riser was actually 50 years and 8 months old at the time of her passing on March 8, 1941.

The death certificate for Goldie Riser fills in a few blanks of those final years of her life. This certificate explains that Goldie passed away from pneumonia after an illness that began on January 20, 1941. It also states Goldie suffered from tuberculosis for five years previous to her passing. Her death certificate is signed by Andy Ballard, who was the caretaker at the Ray County Poor Farm for many years.

A paranormal hot spot in the museum is the basement area, where visitors will discover the eerie remnants of six small prison cells. These cells, with bars on both the windows and the doors, were used during different periods for a variety of reasons. Over time, these cells were home temporarily to Alzheimer's and mentally ill patients until they could be quickly relocated to a state mental hospital. On several occasions, these cells interned criminals awaiting extradition, and, sadly, one of these lonely prison cells held a young juvenile delinquent for nearly a year. Local officials felt a cell at the county poor farm was a far better choice for the young man than having him face the dangers of housing him with adult offenders at a nearby prison.

If the spirit of any former resident would have had a strong enough impression within these cells to leave a lingering presence behind, it would probably be the ghostly remains of wheelchair-bound John Birdie Youngblood. The main resident floors at the poor farm were accessible only by several flights of stairs. In order to be able to take Youngblood outside when needed, he was moved downstairs to live to the basement area. This move also made it easier for the staff to tend to his needs. Here the hallways were just a bit wider, and he could move about slightly more freely than if he had been forced to live above with the other residents.

If spirits of the past can have any influence on the living, they have definitely reached out to former volunteer Rod Fields, who was for quite some time a regular fixture in the building. Rod Fields was not able to stop researching the history of this splendid location. He dedicated countless hours investigating the many lives of those who have passed through the Ray County Poor Farm doors, giving dignity to their troubled and often shortened existence. Much of the information on the background and history of this museum was compiled by Fields and reprinted here as a tribute to this extensive research.

Fields liked to take visitors up to what has been dubbed George's Hall, for it is down the second-floor southwestern hallway that George's ghostly footsteps are most frequently heard. Rod disclosed the following tale:

> One day, while I was standing in the hallway just outside room High School Room and busy looking down the hallway in the other direction, I heard a loud thump coming from inside the room. I rushed inside the room to discover a book, which had been on top of a showcase, sitting in the center of the floor.

He pointed to a glass showcase about four feet high along the northern edge of the wall. "It was this exact book that was lying on the floor." The book has a faded blue bound cover with the words "The Ion 1909" printed in silver on the top. It is a class yearbook from the local high school, the Richmond School. Rod walked over to the showcase and made a point of showing the depth of the metal lip along the edge of the countertop, nearly half an inch thick. Ron continued, "With the edge on the showcase, the book could not have simply slid off of the top. And when I found it, it was all the way in the middle of the room, lying face up as if it was carefully placed there."

Later, while Rod was showing the World War II room on the first floor down an eastern hallway, he began to divulge that this room was yet another location where objects moved across the room unattended, "There are two pictures that are frequently found lying on the floor. They have never broken. We just keep picking them up and putting them back in place." Underneath a brightly colored poster of Rosy the Riveter are two unassuming black-and-white photographs.

Excelsior Springs: Haunted Haven

The first is of a man and woman dressed in white, a husband and wife who both served in the US Navy. Their picture sits on top of a bookcase, propped up against the wall after all attempts to hang it up on a nail were given up long ago. The second traveling portrait is a small black-framed photograph of a soldier in uniform hanging just to the left of the couple in white. No one knows what the ghosts are attempting to relate by moving the pictures and the yearbook about. Are they valued keepsakes of a former resident of the county poor farm? Is the ghost upset about where these items have been placed? Or is it attempting to inform others of its identity? Perhaps we may never know the true motive behind these unexplainable incidents.

The reported stories concerning the moving of objects may fall into one of the most fascinating types of ghostly phenomena, that of an "intelligent haunting." Most intelligent spirits will manifest in physical ways in an attempt to interact with those present at the location. This will include slamming doors, opening and closing windows, cold chills, and a strong presence. A clear description of this type of haunting can be found in Troy Taylor's *The Ghost Hunter's Guidebook*.

One of the strongest examples an intelligent haunting may be occurring at the Ray County Historical Society Museum was an event that took place in the kitchen in front of two eyewitnesses. It was a sunny Saturday afternoon, and director Karen Bush was busy in the kitchen washing dishes and discussing museum business with a member of the board of directors who was seated at the kitchen table across the room. This particular board member had never taken seriously stories of the ghosts at the old county poor farm. Perhaps the ghost decided it was time to make a believer out of the doubting guest, for directly behind Karen Bush the doors of an upper kitchen cabinet slowly and silently opened all by themselves. The frightened guest called Karen's attention to the movement of the cabinet doors. By this time, Karen was so accustomed to the ghosts of her beloved historical site that she was not rattled in the least. Instead, she called to the ghost, saying, "Georgie, go out and make yourself useful by sweeping the sidewalk out front." Immediately the cabinet doors were closed by an unseen hand and all ghostly activity ceased in the building for the remainder of the day. It appears that Georgie the ghost heard and was able to immediately react to Karen's request—although Karen did not report that the front porch had been swept clean.

Margo is another frequent visitor to the Ray County Historical Society. She had found herself one sunny afternoon taking an unexpected nap on one of the front parlor couches. She awoke suddenly and was feeling very embarrassed to be caught napping while a gentleman was taking a tour. Margo states that she clearly saw "a tall black man walking from the parlor down the hall to the military rooms." There was no tour or gentleman in the museum at the time. Research has revealed bits of information regarding a seven-foot-tall African American man named John who had lived in a basement room a long time ago. Before this otherworldly event, Margo had never heard of the former resident named John. The only thing discovered about him to date has been revealed by local residents who remember that John stayed in the rooms below because he was so large and tall that he felt his appearance frightened the residents at the Ray County Poor Farm.

The following excerpt was taken directly from investigation notes compiled by Mitzi Miller after an extensive paranormal investigation at the Ray County Historical Society Museum by the members of the PEDRO research team:

A public investigation was held on a very cold, icy Saturday night in February 2010. The investigation was led by me, Joe Kline, and Mitzi Miller, all members of PEDRO. It was a busy night!

The building has been witness to many deaths and personal traumas. At least 35 people, including Goldie Riser, are known to have died in the building while it was the poor farm between 1910 and 1959. And while it was a nursing home from 1959 to 1971, many more died in the building. Two museum curators have also died in the building, one in the current kitchen and one at the back steps. There has been a lot of emotion and energy imprinted on this location, and it is believed that the paranormal activity is the result of these events.

The group had several experiences that night. The first was on the second floor in the west hallway, when several members distinctly heard the sounds of someone moving around in an area that was unoccupied. This was a loud and clear manifestation of movement witnessed by four people in the investigation.

The second experience also happened in the west hallway in a room displaying costumed mannequins. A motion detector facing the wall was activated by an unknown source. Members began asking questions directed at Goldie, and the K2 EMF (instrument for measuring electromagnetic fields) meter in use began reacting. As more questions were asked, the motion detector continued to react, and the K2 meter continued to flash in sequence of three to four flashings. Then, at the same time, the motion detector and the K2 meter both stopped and did not respond again in that area the rest of the night.

The most interesting part of the investigation took place in the basement, near the cells. As the group was walking through the area, a noticeable temperature drop was felt and then recorded. A dowsing rod session was conducted with Joe holding one set of rods and Mitzi holding the other. It was stated that to answer yes, the rods should cross, and for no, the rods move apart. Based on questions asked and results gotten simultaneously with both sets of rods, it was decided that the entity communicating with the group was a man named John. We had been told of a resident named John, who was a very tall, shy black man who stayed in the basement.

During a follow-up research session in April 2010, Rod Fields took me, Joe, and Mitzi to the cemetery on the museum grounds. This cemetery was used during the time of the poor farm, and the majority of the graves are of people who died while at the poor farm. There are a few people buried here that had no connection to the poor farm. There is only one marker, for a young man who died as a result of a train accident. His family placed the marker.

While we visited the cemetery, Joe picked up several voice clips with his digital recorder. The first is when the group was looking at the marked grave, and Mitzi commented that the man was young. Directly after that there is a clear "yes" from an unknown source. Then, when Rod was telling the story of the young man and his fate with the train, the sound of a train is picked up on the digital recorder but was not heard in real time.

Taking the trip to the Ray County Historical Society Museum is well worth the journey. The drive between Richmond and Excelsior Springs is one of the most picturesque routes in northwestern Missouri, and the museum itself is a treasure trove of historical information and displays. For a bit of fun, one can even stop in the costume shop and try on a few outfits from the past.

Ray County Historical Society Museum
901 West Royal Street
Richmond, MO 64085
Phone: (816) 776-2305
Open year-round, Wednesday–Saturday
10:00 a.m.–4:00 p.m.
www.raycountyhistoricalsociety.com

Tryst Falls is located just north of Excelsior Springs, where rushing waters have created a small waterfall and a gentle pool. This scenic spot, pictured here around the 1950s, was a well-known picnic site even prior to the creation of Excelsior Springs. Ghostly tales at this site surround a slave woman named Annice and events that took place during the summer of 1828. (From the private collection of Betty Bissell.)

TRYST FALLS

A few miles north of Excelsior Springs is Tryst Falls, located on Williams Creek, a tributary of the Fishing River, where the rushing waters have carved into the native limestone, creating a small but splendid, wide, and picturesque waterfall dropping nearly 20 feet to a gentle pool. Small chiseled grooves carved along the falls' rocky eastern embankment are the only traces of a small mill that stood here many years ago. There was also a rock quarry at one time on the east side of the falls.

Over the course of centuries, frequent waters overflowing the banks of the pool have carved out a sheltered area to the west. This peaceful, shaded, grassy spot sits below the eye level of travelers on the nearby road. Its seclusion from the rest of the world is aided by the natural rock outcroppings that wall the area off below the surrounding hillside. This carved-out landscape creates a perfect spot for roasting marshmallows and telling ghost stories as night begins to fall. Complete now with a shelter house, picnic tables, and swings, this scenic spot has been a well-known picnic site to locals even prior to the creation of Excelsior Springs and has become the epicenter of several urban legends.

There are variations to the story, but they are essentially the same legend retold in a similar manner but with different characters in the story's makeup. Tales often begin with a scared and frightened mother sneaking away to the falls in the dead of night with her slumbering infant son wrapped in her arms. Her purpose is clear—she intends to drown the infant by tossing him from the falls into the rushing waters below. Her ghost has been reportedly spotted many times tiptoeing up to the falls, tossing the child in, and hurrying away. Then the air supposedly fills with the sounds of the infant crying loudly as it begins to drown and the screaming wails of its mother as she rushes away.

The tale of the tragedy at Tryst Falls was mentioned briefly in an article appearing in the *Excelsior Springs Daily Standard* on April 22, 1928. The headline reads, "Triple Drowning Which Brought First Hanging of Woman in County Is among Lore around Beautiful Tryst Falls." Unfortunately, the article tells nothing of the story about the drowning itself but touts the beauty, splendor, and history of the site.

Further research into this sad legend led to a more accurate relating of the events. The information was located on page 107 of *History of Clay County from 1822 to 1830*, printed in 1885, with the subtitle, "The First Murder Case." This story was also reprinted in the *History of Clay County* by W.H. Woodson, published in 1920. The title reads, "The First Murder Case—Execution of the Murderess, a Negro Woman." As documented in this history, some time during the summer of 1828 a slave woman named Annice murdered her children at the falls. Annice was a slave belonging to a man only identified as Mr. Prior, who lived near Greenville, Missouri. The article reports that she decoyed her children to a small stream. She threw two (or three) of her youngest children into a deep pool formed by a small waterfall. When she was discovered, she was chasing after her oldest child. Annice was then arrested and indicted. This brief retelling of the events states only that next she was tried before a jury. Judge David Todd sentenced her to be hanged on August 23. The article continues, "The wretched creature was hung on the day appointed, by Col. Shubael Allen, sheriff." The article ends with the statement, "The execution came off in the northern part of Liberty."

The tragic trial of Annice did not take place in the historic Liberty Court House, which stands majestically in the center of nearby Liberty Square. The following excerpt from page 103 of the *History of Clay County from 1822 to 1830* explains, "February 11, 1822, the first county court of Clay County convened at the house of John Owens, which stood on what is now lot 186, on the northwest corner of Water and Mill streets, in the city of Liberty." The publication further states, "There was no fixed place for holding court, it being sometimes held under the arbor of a tree, until 1832, when the first court house was built." We may never know the exact location of the trial and hanging of poor Annice. Perhaps future investigators and researchers will uncover this information along with her final resting place.

Assistance with research is gratefully accredited to the Clay County Museum and Historical Society.

Tryst Falls Park
Route 92
Excelsior Springs, MO 64024
Open during daylight hours

Unidentified Flying Objects

The year was 1966, and according to many newspapers and Air Force reports, a UFO craze was sweeping the nation. In every major city in the United States, reports of flying saucers were given to local police at an alarming rate—far more than had been reported previously or has since. This book will not try to explain why that year saw such a dramatic increase in unidentified objects in the skies, simply that this phenomena also took place in large numbers in the Midwest and in particular in the airspace over Excelsior Springs.

In one year, over 1,000 UFO sightings were reported in the area. Amazing stories were printed in the local newspapers. UFO watch parties were formed, and local residents gathered on the hillsides to keep a watchful eye on the skies above. Respected citizens came forward with their own tales of otherworldly visitations.

One local resident of good reputation gave this report when questioned on the many sightings of the times. Gloria Bingham O'Dell, a former newspaper reporter for the *Excelsior Springs Daily Standard*, gave the following interview:

> My family lived outside of town back in those days, and the homes were pretty far apart. I remember clearly that it was getting close to nightfall. We had all just finished supper, and I was standing at the kitchen sink washing dishes. I could see the field to the south of our home through the window in front of me.
>
> You can imagine my surprise when I saw, about 150 yards from my window, a spaceship coming down and hovering over the fields. It was silver and saucer shaped, just like in the movies. I can only guess that its size was over 50 feet across. I'd say it was out there over the wheat crops for a good 5 to 10 minutes. I was able to notice tiny white lights along the underside. They were blinking on and off in a regular pattern.
>
> The ship was there long enough for me to call everyone together to come and have a good look at it. Then all of a sudden there was a whooshing sound, and the ship went straight up into the sky. It hovered in the air, way up high for just a moment or two, then shot off sideways and out of sight beyond the horizon. I've never seen anything like it in my life before or since.

Surprisingly, when Gloria was asked about ghosts in Excelsior Springs, she said that she had never heard of any place in town that was haunted.

BIBLIOGRAPHY

elmsresort.com/about/history

Excelsior Springs Chamber of Commerce. *Excelsior Springs, America's Haven of Health*. Excelsior Springs, MO: Excelsior Springs Chamber of Commerce, 1930. Excelsior Springs, MO: Excelsior Springs Centennial History Book Boosters, 1974.

Excelsior Springs Daily Standard, February 15–July 1940.

History of Clay and Platte Counties. St. Louis, MO: National Historical Company, O.P. Williams & Co., publisher, 1885.

McGrane, Martin. *The James Farm, Its People, Their Lives, Their Times*. Madison, SD: Caleb Perkins Press, 2006.

Proffitt, Barbara, Carol Proffitt, and M. Virginia Mills. *Clevenger Families of Ray County, Missouri*. Cullman, AL: The Gregath Publishing Company, 1991.

Schondelmeyer, Brent. *Building a First Class Bank, The Story of UMB*. Kansas City, MO: UMB Financial Corporation, 1986.

Soltysiak, Harry. *Reflections of Excelsior Springs*. Marceline, MO: Heritage House Publishing Company, Inc., 1992.

Southall, Richard. *How to Be a Ghost Hunter*. St. Paul, MN: Llewellyn Worldwide, 2003.

Stiles, T.J. *Jesse James, Last Rebel of the Civil War*. New York: Vintage House Books, 2003.

Taylor, Troy. *The Ghost Hunter's Guidebook*. Alton, IL: Whitechapel Productions Press, 2001.

The Waters of Excelsior Springs, Valley of Vitality. Excelsior Springs, MO: Excelsior Springs Spa Development, 2003.

Wilda, Sandy and Larry K. Hancks. *Stalking Louis Curtiss, Architect: A Portrait of the Man and His Work*. Kansas City, MO: Ward Parkway Printing, 1991.

www.eshpc.org.

www.theidlehour.com

INDEX

About Excelsior Springs Museum and Archives

The Excelsior Springs Museum and Archives got its start in the Clay County State Bank, which was built in 1906 of Bedford sandstone and designed by architect Louis Curtiss. It was done in a Renaissance style with Roman classic details with two massive columns in the front. The interior details include beautiful marble floors and a 28-foot electrically lighted arched plaster ceiling. The original vault at the south end has its massive circular steel door. This type of design represents safety, strength, and durability and in its day the prosperity and progress taking place in Excelsior Springs.

The building was enlarged in the 1920s, and the front facade received alterations in the 1950s, including removing the steps to make the building handicap accessible and enclosing the entryway between the columns. It was during the 1920s expansion that the painted murals *The Angelus* and *The Gleaners* were added to the north and south upper walls. They were done by Count Edmund deSzaak of Budapest, Hungary.

In 1968, the Kemper family of Kansas City, Missouri, gifted the building to the City of Excelsior Springs. After a short transfer of ownership to the local chamber of commerce, the building is now owned by the Excelsior Springs Museum and Archives. In 2005, the museum acquired the building next door on the east side of the museum, which was formerly the Francis Hotel. With local help, it was rehabbed into additional space for exhibits and an art gallery. In 2010, there was even an art school in the space. In the basement of the Francis exhibit hall is a newspaper archive going back over 100 years. It is this archive that allows us to do a great deal of research for those in and out of the area.

The charter for the Excelsior Springs Museum and Archives was issued on December 6, 1967, as the Excelsior Historical Museum with 101 charter members. All museum work is done by volunteers, and the museum receives no outside sources of money. It is an entirely self-sufficient endeavor. Its mission is "to collect and preserve the history of the City of Excelsior Springs, Missouri, to maintain museum buildings, and to provide information regarding people who have resided in the community."

The volunteers work hard to rotate exhibits, collect the history of people of the area, and do research for those requesting it. Each year, a "founding family" is honored with a special exhibit. A garden tour is held each summer, and the volunteers work hard at finding other ways to raise money in support of the museum. For several years now, the museum has had a traveling exhibit; these are always well-attended events. We also have people who come from all over the world to examine our museum and our processes. The board of directors is a working one, and many of them volunteer in several areas of museum activity. There is always something to do, and we are always seeking good people to volunteer their time and talent.

www.arcadiapublishing.com

Discover books about the town where you grew up, the cities where your friends and families live, the town where your parents met, or even that retirement spot you've been dreaming about. Our Web site provides history lovers with exclusive deals, advanced notification about new titles, e-mail alerts of author events, and much more.

MADE IN THE

Arcadia Publishing, the leading local history publisher in the United States, is committed to making history accessible and meaningful through publishing books that celebrate and preserve the heritage of America's people and places. Consistent with our mission to preserve history on a local level, this book was printed in South Carolina on American-made paper and manufactured entirely in the United States.

This book carries the accredited Forest Stewardship Council (FSC) label and is printed on 100 percent FSC-certified paper. Products carrying the FSC label are independently certified to assure consumers that they come from forests that are managed to meet the social, economic, and ecological needs of present and future generations.

FSC
Mixed Sources
Product group from well-managed forests and other controlled sources

Cert no. SW-COC-001530
www.fsc.org
© 1996 Forest Stewardship Council

Find Your Place in History.